WWII JEEP GUIDEBOOK

Buying, Owning and Enjoying Your WWII jeep

Ren Bernier

Picture Credits
All images by Ren Bernier except:

Fig. 02, 03, 04, 05, 19, 45, 46, 50, 55, 64, 65, 103 - U.S. Army, Fig. 06, 07, 09, 15, 51, 93 - Frank Berg, Fig. 10, 13 - Michael Danieli , Fig. 22 – Mark Tombleson, Fig. 26 – Alexander Bernier, Fig. 34, 35, 36, 37 – Greg Malcervelli, Fig. 49 – Ron Fitzpatrick, Fig. 52, 87 – Joe Hall, Fig. 53 - MD Juan, Inc., Fig. 61 – Jon Rogers, Fig. 75 – State of Maine Bureau of Motor Vehicles, Fig. 94, 96, 97, 99, 100, 101, 102 – John Barton, Fig. 95, 98 – Bill Oakes

Bernier, Ren
WWII jeep Guidebook: Buying, Owning and Enjoying Your WWII jeep
p. 126
1. WWII—Non-Fiction. 2. Hobby—Non-Fiction.
3. Auto—Non-Fiction 4. Auto Restoration—Non-Fiction
1. Title.

ISBN 978-1-0882-0589-1

Printed by
Pejepscot Publishing
Topsham, Maine

Printed in the United States of America

First Just Write Books Edition 2005
First Pejepscot Publishing Edition 2024

Acknowledgements

Putting this information together made me realize how much the WWII jeep hobby has influenced my life. Because of my interest in restoring, owning and enjoying old jeeps over the course of thirty odd years I have learned a lot of mechanical skills and techniques and I have bought and sold more jeeps and parts than I can remember. Each sale involved meeting someone I wouldn't have otherwise met. I have traveled up and down the east coast and across America to California attending Military Vehicle Meets because of the WWII jeep. I learned to build a website and developed it into a busy spot for jeep restorers, again, because of WWII jeeps. I have made great friends from across town, across America, and as far off as Norway, Australia and New Zealand. Because of the WWII jeep I have heard stories from WWII veterans that have given me great respect for that "Greatest Generation". Because of the WWII jeep I have traveled the remote woods roads of northern Maine. I have given talks at museums, written articles for magazines and visited the Smithsonian Institution's storage facilities, all because of the WWII jeep. What a wonderful, life-long hobby that I have found in this ugly little vehicle from a war long ago. Because of the WWII jeep I have even written this book. Wow, what a hobby.

The preparation of this book was made possible with help from a lot of friends. In particular I want to thank Stephen Hatch for his help in proofreading and editing the text and images in this book. I also want to thank Joe Hall of Vintage Wiring of Maine who taught me much of what I wrote in this book.

I have learned something about WWII jeeps from Mike Quinn, Tony Norton, Ron Fitzpatrick, Jon Rogers, Alasdair Brass, Frank Berg, Michael Danieli, Daryl Deppe, Jim Gilmore, Frank Buck, Bill Spear, Mike Seymour, John Barton, Greg Malcervelli, Jim Kilbourne, Chuck Lutz, Bill Hollinger, Paul Fitzgerald, Mark Tombleson, Robert Notman, Tom Wolbolt, Bill Hawley, Joe Potter, Jon Schneider, Doug Page, Bill Campbell, George Baxter, Pete DeBella, Mark Dodd, Garrick Smith, Bill Keen, Dave Pizzoferrato, Sheldon Greene, Richard Grace, Ernie Baals, Joel Bernier, Dave Aro, Craig Cakouros, Charles Pelkey, Mark Baker, Mike Wright, Mac McCluskey, Howard Widman, Marc Open and many others. Thank You.

I also want to thank Mike Arman for the idea about the book and especially my wife, Stephanie, for the encouragement to do it, and for being patient with me while I did.

Ren Bernier,
Topsham, Maine June 2005

From *Websters New Collegiate Dictionary*, copyright 1981 by G.&C.. Merriam Co.

jeep \'jep\ *n*,: a small general-purpose motor vehicle with an 80 inch wheelbase, 1/4 – ton capacity and four-wheel drive used by the US Army in World War II

Jeep *trademark* – used for a civilian automotive vehicle

The distinction above is the capitalization of the "j" in the word "jeep"

Jeep is a registered trademark of DaimlerChrysler Corp.(DCC)

Note that this book is not a DaimlerChrysler publication. It has not been sponsored, endorsed, reviewed, or authorized by Daimler-Chrysler. If you have questions contact the author, not Daimler-Chrysler. All information is believed to be accurate, but is used at your own risk.

www.wwiijeepbook.com

TABLE OF CONTENTS

Appendixes

Photo Credits

All images by Ren Bernier except:

Fig. 02, 03, 04, 05, 19, 45, 46, 50, 55, 64, 65, 103–U.S. Army,
Fig. 06, 07, 09, 15, 51, 93–Frank Berg,
Fig. 10, 13–Michael Danieli,
Fig. 22–Mark Tombleson,
Fig. 26–Alexander Bernier,
Fig. 34, 35, 36, 37–Greg Malcervelli,
Fig. 49–Ron Fitzpatrick,
Fig. 52, 87–Joe Hall, Fig. 53 MD Juan, Inc.,
Fig. 61–Jon Rogers,
Fig. 75–State of Maine Bureau of Motor Vehicles,
Fig. 94, 96, 97, 99, 100, 101, 102–John Barton,
Fig. 95, 98–Bill Oakes

INTRODUCTION

Perhaps it began when you were a kid and you read in the back of *Boy's Life* magazine about those "jeeps-in-a-crate" that could be had for a mere $50. Or maybe it was a steady diet of *Rat Patrol* episodes on TV with jeeps tearing across the sand dunes, machine guns blaring. Was it your father's or your grandfather's stories about "his" jeep in WWII and how it faithfully outperformed it's expectations over and over again? However the idea was initiated, for many of us, the desire to have a WWII jeep goes far back. With the recent recognition finally given to the "Greatest Generation" and the associated interest in WWII history, many people are interested in having a WWII jeep of their own.

Too often we hear of persons buying a "restored" WWII jeep from an unscrupulous or uninformed source only to end up disappointed with their purchase. Restoring a jeep on your own can be a satisfying process, but it requires skill, time and money—and selecting a good candidate vehicle for restoration is crucial. Driving

Fig 01 – *The author's 1942 GPW on a woodlot access road.*

and maintaining a 60 year old vehicle is very different from owning a modern automobile and requires extra care to protect and preserve your investment and your safety.

A WWII jeep is slow, noisy, uncomfortable, cold in the winter, hot in the summer, and wet when it rains. It has no stereo, no heater, no legroom and very little horsepower. In spite of this, few vehicles are as much fun to drive—why?

A WWII jeep has no chrome, no shine, no decorative features at all and yet I have boxes full of first-place trophies from local car shows where I was surrounded by acres of chrome and shine. Individuals, families, young and old, walked past the row after row of gorgeous show cars to look over and spend time with my homely little jeep—why?

When given a choice, a WWII jeep is selected by veterans in parades over shiny Cadillac convertibles as their preferred "ride of honor"—Why?

The reasons why the above observations are fact can be argued at length, but I feel that the underlying reason why the WWII jeep is so loved is it's honesty. It is a truly honest vehicle.

A jeep doesn't pretend to be anything that it isn't. It does not claim to be comfortable or fast, but it WILL get you from point A to point B, guaranteed, even if there is no road between A and B. The WWII jeep's design is plain and simple—and understandable. It doesn't hide anything behind chrome or fins. It looks the way it does for a very practical reason, and that is a refreshing bit of integrity in design. The jeep's honesty in its claims have been fully substantiated by it's service record in WWII and beyond. The Veterans who choose it over the comfortable Cadillac for the parade remember the jeep's role and respect it for what it did for them.

Its simple, robust design gave the WWII jeep a legendary reliability in the field. The jeep served well beyond it's intended purpose acting as not only a Reconnaissance Car, but as weapons platform, ambulance, troop transport, equipment hauler, tractor, railroad locomotive (when fitted with special wheels) and more. The flat hood served equally well as a dinner table, operating table, map table or altar in the field. It was beloved by the troops and remains one of the most recognizable vehicles in the world.

This book is intended to be a guide for the jeep enthusiast interested in buying, owning and driving an authentic WWII jeep. As with all pursuits, knowledge is power. The old adage to "look before you leap" is good advice, but only so if you know what you are looking at. It is my hope that you, the reader, can use the information in this book to make a wise decision in your WWII jeep selection, operation and care.

CHAPTER 1
General Overview of the WWII jeep

Development History

To become an informed WWII jeep buyer or owner involves studying bit of history. WWII history of sorts...

On September 23, 1940 in response to an Army Invitation For Bids, the American Bantam Car Company of Butler, Pa. delivered a prototype vehicle to Camp Holabird for testing. The test vehicle was immediately recognized by the Army as one of the most important and innovative vehicles in the history of modern land warfare. Delivered and tested as Bantam Reconnaissance Car #1001, it was soon thereafter that it's testers dubbed it the "jeep".

Though the design and development of the first prototype jeep was primarily the work of Bantam Car Co., both Willys and Ford later supplied prototypes to the Army also. The Army tested all three designs and ultimately settled on one standardized jeep design.

Fig 02 – *Bantam's prototype jeep poses for a picture with its builders in late September, 1940.*

The initial contract for these standardized jeeps, model MB, was awarded to Willys in October, 1941. With America's entry into WWII seeming imminent, the

> *A common misconception is that the letters "GPW" stood for General Purpose-Willys, but this is incorrect. The letters "GPW" are from Ford's own vehicle model codes where "G" indicated Government contract, "P" was Ford's code for an 80" wheelbase Reconnaissance Car 4X4, and "W" meant Willys design motor.*

Army felt that a second producer of jeeps would be needed. Ford Motor Company was contracted to build standardized jeeps based on the Willys MB design. Ford's designation for their standardized jeeps was model GPW.

Willys and Ford went on to produce approximately 650,000 standardized jeeps between November 1941 and August 1945. Ford stopped producing jeeps with the end of WWII, but Willys adopted the jeep name and developed many successful civilian versions of the trusty wartime jeep.

Let's summarize this. Before November, 1941 there were three different manufacturers of prototype jeep designs: American Bantam Car Co. (Bantam BRC40), Ford Motor Co. (Ford GP), and Willys-Overland Co. (Willys MA). These vehicles are each different from the standardized WWII jeep. They are relatively rare and represent less

***Fig 03** – The Bantam BRC40 in early 1941.*

***Fig 04** – The Willys MA.*

***Fig 05** – The Ford GP.*

than 1.5% of all the jeeps built before the end of WWII.

The WWII jeep that veterans and the public remember and recognize are the so-called standardized WWII jeeps—the Willys MB and Ford GPW. These standardized WWII jeeps were built from November 1941 through August 1945 only. While a prototype jeep is a valuable and historically interesting piece, it is beyond the scope of this book.

When production of Willys MB's and Ford GPWs ended in August of 1945, Willys redesigned the standardized MB into a "civilianized" model, the CJ2A. Willys-Overland (and their successors—Kaiser and American Motors) continued to build jeeps for civilian markets, the CJ series of jeeps, from late 1945 on. Willys and others also built jeeps for the US government during the Korean conflict (M38 jeeps) and Vietnam conflicts (M151 jeeps). While it seems obvious, it is important to remember that actual WWII jeeps were *only* built during WWII.

Interestingly, after WWII a French company purchased much of the Willys WWII jeep tooling and built standardized jeeps well after WWII, into the 1960's in fact. Willys of France (WoF) built these "Hotchkiss" jeeps for the French government for many years and a considerable amount of WoF parts are still available which interchange with standardized WWII jeep parts.

Buyers and sellers often confuse civilian and other post WWII jeeps for actual WWII standardized jeeps. While cj2a's, cj3a's, and M38's share many design concepts with the original WWII jeeps, they are, in fact, very different. At first glance it would appear that a cj2a is simply a WWII jeep with a different grille (seven slots instead of the nine slots of the WWII model), but there are essentially no *identical* parts between the two models. Certainly many parts will interchange, but a trained eye can spot a civilian part on a WWII jeep with ease.

So we have jeep prototypes built before the war, a half-million standardized jeeps built during WWII, and a large variety of civilian and military jeep models built in the 60 years since WWII ended. To simplify our task I will divide all these jeeps into two major groups: WWII jeeps and "all the rest". Henceforth we will be

Fig 06 – *A row of restored standardized WWII jeeps.*

concerned with WWII jeeps only—and we very well may find *that* to be confusing enough!

Manufacturers, Models and Major Changes

The WWII jeep evolved as the war progressed. There are numerous differences between the first and last standardized Willys MBs built. Some of these differences are subtle, some of these differences are obvious. To further complicate the matter, the Ford GPW is different from the Willys in almost every part (by design), and yet every part is interchangeable (also by design). The GPW evolved with time, too. An early GPW is different from a late-war GPW. Couple all this with the fact that during WWII many service depots were disassembling and reassembling jeeps in rebuild programs with no concern for whether the jeep was a Ford or Willys, or had "early-war" or "late-war" details and the result is that two authentic and accurate WWII jeeps side-by-side may have very different details throughout.

Standardized WWII jeeps

Slat-Grill MBs

From November 1941 until around mid February of 1942, only Willys was producing standardized jeeps, the Willys MB. These first MBs are often referred to as the "Slat-grill" MBs because their most distinguishing feature is an iron-bar type grille. The grill was a welded-up affair consisting of many individual pieces of flat steel stock arc-welded together. It was a very labor-intensive process to fabricate and was replaced by the Ford-designed stamped steel grill we are most familiar with in January, 1942. Other distinguish-

Another common misconception is that the name "jeep" was derived from a slurring of the letters "GP", but the word "jeep" was in common usage as early as 1938 - two years before the first jeep appeared. Exactly how the little 4x4 Reconnaissance Car ended up with the name "jeep" has never really been determined.

ing features of the very early slat grill MBs include the name "Willys" embossed into the lower left corner of the rear panel, a square-cornered fuel tank sump, no glove box in the dashboard, and solid-disc wheels. Many more subtle differences ex-

Fig 07 – *Willys MB slat grill serial number MB119284.*

ist, but certainly the slat-type grill, lack of glovebox and the embossed rear panel are the most obvious features allowing a jeep enthusiast to spot a "slattie" from 50 feet away.

Approximately 20,000 slat grill MBs were produced in Willys' Toledo, Ohio facility. These early MBs are amongst the most desirable of the standardized WWII jeeps and can command higher prices both as restored vehicles and as unrestored original vehicles when compared with more common later-war jeeps. Slat Grill jeeps represent less than 10% of the jeeps produced by Willys, and less than 5% of all WWII jeeps produced.

Early MBs

During the first half of 1942 Willys MBs adopted many improvements that Ford also included in their early GPWs. MBs built during this time now had gloveboxes, a rounded fuel tank sump, two-piece "combat" rims, a one-piece stamped grill. The MBs built at this time also retained the embossed "Willys" in their rear panels, and are often referred to as "Willys scripts" even though the term "script" refers to the script style of font used on the classic Ford logo.

Ford "Script" GPWs

By February of 1942, Ford Motor Company had begun production of the GPW. Like the early Willys jeeps, early Ford jeeps also had the manufacturer name embossed into the lower left corner of the rear panel. This practice continued with Ford GPWs through mid July of 1942. The early Ford script GPWs sported the new and improved stamped grill, a glovebox, and two-piece "combat" rims. Neither Ford GPWs nor Willys MBs built during this time came from the factory with spare gas can carriers on the rear panels; this feature was added to standardized jeep production in the summer of 1942. The absence of the spare gas can allowed a clear

Fig 08 – Ford "script" stamping on the rear panel of an April 1942 GPW.

view of the embossed "Willys" or "Ford" on the rear panels of these early jeeps, but the military added gas cans to most of these jeeps in the field as an approved "Field Modification". Nonetheless, the embossed rear panels were deleted from both the MB and the GPW by July of 1942.

About 40,000 Ford Script GPWs were built in all. When compared to later-war standardized jeeps, Ford (and Willys) script models generally command higher prices.

"Pure" Ford and Willys WWII jeeps

By this point in time, late 1942, the visual differences between Ford-built and Willys-built jeeps were becoming less and less obvious. The major visual differences between the two manufacturers vehicles were found in the structural configuration

Fig 09 – A restored late-war composite-bodied Ford GPW.

of their bodies and frames. Ford Motor Company was manufacturing their own jeep bodies and Willys-Overland was having it's bodies manufactured for them by American Central Manufacturing (ACM). These mid-production jeeps are sometimes referred to as "pure" Ford or "pure" Willys WWII jeeps because each carried their manufacturers body design.

Composite-Bodied jeeps

The era of the "pure" Ford or "pure" Willys WWII jeeps ended in early 1944 when a single body design, built by a single manufacturer, ACM, was adopted. This new body design retained features from both manufacturer's original designs and is known as a "composite" body design because it is a combination of structural configurations. ACM built composite bodies for both Willys and Ford jeeps throughout the end of WWII further obscuring the visual differences between these late-war MB and GPWs.

In Summary

Gradual design changes to the WWII jeep happened more or less continually throughout the war, but a few major styles of each manufacturer's vehicles can be identified.

In the case of Willys MBs, four main styles emerge:
- slat-grille MBs (Nov '41–Jan '42)
- early MBs (Jan '42–July '42)
- mid-production pure Willys MBs (August '42–Jan '44)
- late-production, composite bodied MBs (Jan '44–Aug '45).

Ford GPWs are easily grouped into three main styles:
- early "Script" GPWs (Jan '42–July '42)
- mid-production pure Ford GPWs (August '42–Jan '44)
- late-production, composite bodied GPWs (Jan '44–Aug '45).

These groupings are an oversimplification of the jeep's evolutionary development, but for our purposes having four styles of MBs and three styles of GPWs will work.

WWII jeep Details

Serial Numbers

Why is the WWII jeep's serial number important? Besides serving as the VIN, important for titling and registering the vehicle, the vehicle's serial numbers can provide additional information about the vehicle itself. MBs were assigned serial numbers in chronological order starting with the first MB built in late 1941 at serial number MB100001, then MB100002, and so on. GPWs were also chronologically numbered starting in February, 1942 with GPW1, then GPW2 and so on. By knowing the vehicle's serial number we can determine an approximate date of manufacture. (see appendix)

Furthermore, the serial number can be used to provide information about the motor that is found in a particular MB or GPW. Upon assembly of a GPW chassis, Ford Motor Company assembly plants (there were five plants producing GPWs) would stamp the already-assigned motor number onto the frame rail creating the vehicle serial number. Therefore, GPW motor numbers exactly matched the vehicle serial numbers when the jeep left the factory. A GPW that retains its original "matching numbers" motor is often a more valuable piece to a collector.

MB engines and frames were sequentially numbered independently. The MB frames were fabricated in one facility and numbered sequentially as they were built. The engines for MBs were assembled and sequential serial numbers were applied to these in a different facility. When the frames and the engines were brought together in the final assembly of the vehicle, the frame and engine were paired up without regard to their numbers. As a result, MBs left the factory with non-matching engine and frame numbers. An MB's engine number is higher sequentially than its frame number because numerous MB engines were removed from the sequence for other applications during the war causing a gap between the higher engine number and the frame number. The magnitude of this "gap" increased as the war progressed.

In addition to vehicle (frame) serial numbers and engine numbers, the bodies of MBs and later GPWs were numbered. The bodies on early and mid-production MBs with Willys-style bodies were numbered sequentially when built. This body number, stamped into the body toeboard

Fig 10 – WWII jeep data plates. A) Gearshift pattern for the transmission and transfer case. B) Vehicle-specific data showing serial number, date of delivery, vehicle weight, etc. C) Caution plate listing maximum permissible speeds for each gear.

Fig 11a – Ford GPW frame serial number stamping location is on the top of the frame rail as indicated by the arrow.

Fig 12a – Willys MB frame serial number tag location.

*Fig 11b – Close-up of the ford GPW frame serial number. The serial number starts and ends with a star that is not visible in picture (*GPW20577*)*

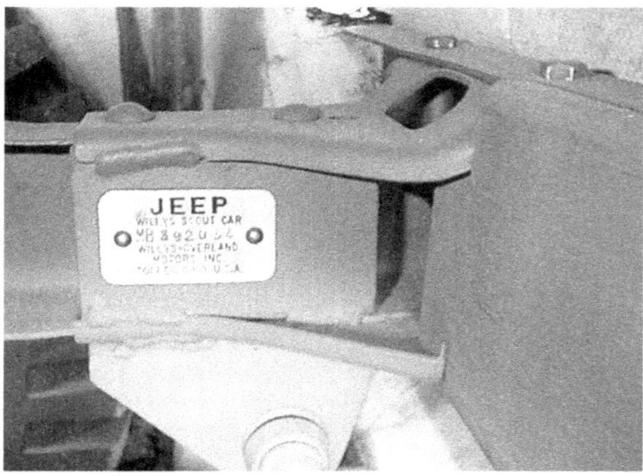

Fig 12b – Close-up of a late-war MB serial number tag. The earlier MBs used a simple, smaller tag as seen in Fig 20.

brace by American Central Manufacturing (ACM) was independent of both the frame and the engine number, but loosely related to them both. Essentially, the earlier the MB, the lower the body number. Early Ford-built bodies were not numbered. At the beginning of 1944, when both Ford and Willys adopted the ACM-built "composite" bodies, ACM started the numbering sequence at body number one again and from this point on both Ford and Willys jeeps sported numbered bodies.

Data Plates

There are three data plates on the GPW and MB glovebox doors. The center plate has the vehicle identification information including Manufacturer, Model, Serial Number, and Date of Delivery which is assumed to be the date of manufacture. If these plates are painted over be very careful in removing the paint as valuable information about the vehicle could easily be lost.

The serial number from the frame was stamped onto the data plate once the vehicle was assembled. If a WWII jeep's data plate is missing the serial number can still be found, with luck, by looking on the frame itself. (Fig. 10)

GPW Serial Number Stamped on Frame

The GPW frame is stamped with the serial number in this format: GPW123456. This stamping can be found on the top of the left frame rail and is visible in the engine compartment just forward of the engine mount bracket. The stamping is typically very light so some care may be required to prevent damage. (Fig. 11a,11b)

MB Serial Number on the Frame

The MB frame has a tag that is stamped with the serial number in this format: MB123456. This tag can be found on the inside of the left frame rail just behind the bumper. It is a small metal tag that

Fig 14 – *Toeboard gussets used on slat-grill, early and mid-production "Pure Willys" MBs. The arrow shows the location of the body number stamping applied by the body manufacturer, ACM. (see also Fig 22)*

is held in place with two small rivet pins. The number on this tag should match the number found on the data plate, but it will not match the engine serial number.

I have noticed that on the font used to stamp these frame serial number tags the numeral "1" often appears as "I" on earlier MBs in particular (i.e., "MB105432" looks like "MB I05432")—don't let this confuse you! (Fig. 12a, 12b)

Motor Number

GPW engines are stamped with the serial number in this format: GPW123456. This stamping can be found on a rounded boss that is on the right side of the engine near the front of the block just below the head. It is under the oil filter canister. On GPWs, this number should exactly match both the data plate and frame numbers if

Fig 13 – *The engine serial number location on both GPW and MB motors built during WWII. Normally this stamping is partially obscured by the oil filter.*

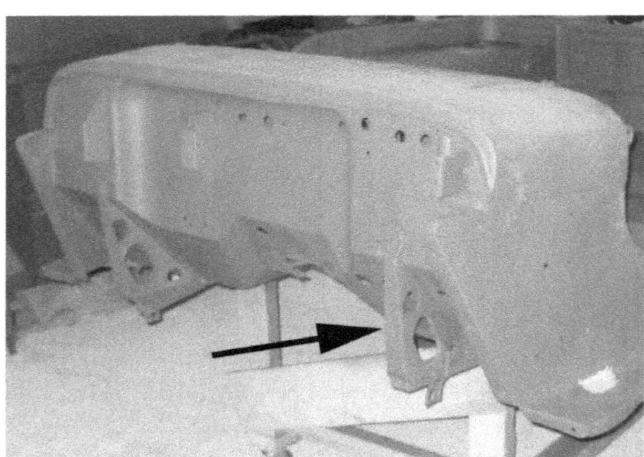

Fig 15 – Toeboard gussets on an ACM Type II "composite" body. These gussets are the same as those used in Ford-built bodies. The arrow shows the location of the ACM Type II body number that is stamped on the face of the gusset.

the original engine is still in the vehicle. (Fig. 13)

The MB engine is stamped with the serial number in this format: MB123456. This stamping is also found on a rounded boss that is on the right side of the engine near the front of the block just below the head. On MBs, this number does not match either the data plate or frame numbers even if the original engine is still in the vehicle

Body Numbers

The Ford-built GPW bodies did not have a body number stamped on them. This changed when Ford began using bodies built for them by American Central Manufacturing (ACM Type II body) at the beginning of 1944. These ACM GPW body tubs were stamped with a serial number in this format: 123456. This stamping can be found on the driver's side toeboard gusset which is a triangular brace on the body tub best viewed from in the engine compartment. On GPWs, this number does not match either the data plate, frame numbers, or engine number.

The MB body tub is stamped with a serial number in this format: 123456.

This stamping can be found on the driver's side toeboard gusset which is a triangular brace on the body tub best viewed from in the engine compartment. On MBs, this number does not match either the data plate, frame numbers, or engine number. These body numbers on MBs start at approximately body number 2000 in the late fall of 1941, but the numbering sequence restarts at 1 in early January of 1944 with the adoption of the ACM Type II "composite" body. (Fig. 14, 15)

Hood Numbers

The prominent hood numbers, or U.S.A. numbers seen stenciled on either side of the hood on WWII jeeps are more correctly known as "registration numbers". These numbers were applied by painted stencil in light blue drab paint by the manufacturer once the finished vehicles were accepted by the US military. The arm of the US government responsible for buying jeeps from the manufacturers, the Quartermaster Corps (QMC) early in the war and later the Ordnance Department (ORD) employed inspectors at both Willys and Ford plants who were responsible for testing and accepting each finished vehicle. Once the vehicles passed inspection/testing, they were assigned a registration

Fig 16 – Registration numbers and the cowl "S". The periods used on the U.S.A. should be square, not round. These markings are to be applied with blue drab paint.

number that started with the numerals "20" which signified 1/4 ton 4X4 reconnaissance car such as "U.S.A. 20100234". These accepted vehicles were stenciled in batches as they were produced and tested so the registration numbers tend to increase with increasing magnitude of serial number, but because vehicles were stenciled in batches, the relationship is not exactly 1:1. Apparently, once a vehicle passed inspection it was sent to a lot where the accepted vehicles were accumulated. Periodically, a stenciler would apply the registration numbers to the vehicles in the accumulation lot before they were shipped off. The stenciler would most likely walk up and down rows of parked vehicles applying registration numbers without regard to the vehicle's serial numbers. Furthermore, the QMC or ORD assigned different batches of registration numbers to Ford and Willys to use at their facilities and so, depending on production rates, some facilities might use their allocated registration numbers more quickly than another facility. These procedures caused the registration numbers to fall out of sequence both with respect to serial number as well as date of delivery.

Most WWII jeep hood numbers included an additional character of "S". This "S" was normally located on the cowl

Fig 17 – *Army regulations permitted a GI to name his vehicle and specified this area above the rear wheel for application of vehicle names.*

Fig 18 – *Individual unit markings as specified by AR-850. These markings are for the 9th Infantry division, 47th Infantry, Company E, vehicle number one. The stars' sizes and locations are also specified by AR-850. These markings are to be applied with white drab paint.*

of the jeep and signified that the vehicle had passed a radio noise suppression test. Upon repainting of a jeep in service, the cowl "S" was often times simply appended to the hood number itself such as "U.S.A. 20135771-S". Very early jeep hood numbers began with a prefix letter of "W" signifying "War Department", but the "W" was dropped in late 1941.

Pale blue drab paint was used for factory-applied registration numbers throughout most of the war with a change to flat white paint late in 1945.

Other Markings

Other markings, letters, numerals, stars, etc. found on jeeps in WWII service constitute the individual unit markings that were applied in the field. These markings varied considerably even though Army regulations manual AR850 specified the details of location, size, color, etc. of all of these. These markings were applied in hundreds of different locations by a wide variety of service personnel with widely

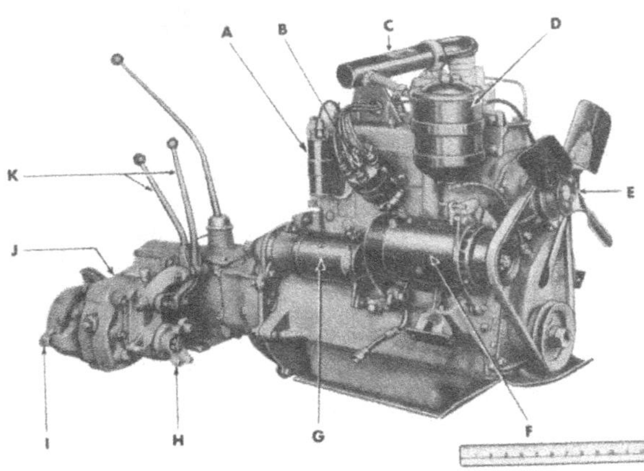

Fig 19 – The WWII jeep powerplant. The Go-Devil engine and T-84 transmission.

varying conditions to work under. As a result, factory applied registration numbers are much more consistent in quality, font and location than unit markings are. Unit markings are normally applied using drab white paint and cut stencils. Reprints of AR850 are available if you want to decode or reproduce certain markings on any particular jeep.

Engine

The standardized WWII jeep was equipped with a 60 horsepower, 134 cubic inch 4 cylinder L-head engine known as a "Go-Devil" engine. The engine was an improved Willys design that was first used on Willys automobiles in the 1930's. It is

Fig 20 – This tubular front crossmember identifies this as a Willys MB frame. Note the early style MB serial number tag on the front frame horn.

Fig 21 – The inverted "U" style front frame crossmember used on Ford GPW frames.

a simple and reliable motor and parts are readily available for it today. The Ford GPW used a Ford-manufactured version of the same engine with all parts interchangeable with its Willys counterpart. The Willys MB engine and the Ford GPW engine look identical at first glance, and only with close observation can the jeep enthusiast distinguish between the two. Furthermore, many post-war Willys vehicles were equipped with essentially the same engine with a gear-driven instead of a chain-driven camshaft. Close inspection can identify a post-war "Go-Devil" quite readily however.

The most reliable way to identify a WWII era Go Devil is to examine the engine's serial number. MB and GPW engines have serial numbers stamped on the right-hand side of the block on a raised boss and the numbers begin with the prefix "MB" or "GPW". Post-war blocks have the serial number stamped on the top surface of the block directly above the water pump on the front of the engine. While a post-war cj2a, cj3a, or M38 engine will interchange with an original MB or GPW engine, a WWII jeep with an "incorrect" post war engine installed is less valuable to a collector.

In addition to a stamped engine serial number, both MB and GPW engines were cast with casting codes, date marks, assembly dates and other information. The engine serial number can determine, with certainty in the case of a GPW, and within a reasonable likelihood in the case

  WWII JEEP GUIDEBOOK

Fig 22 – *Angular, multi-piece floor bracing used on slat-grill, early and mid-production pure Willys WWII jeeps. These bodies, built for Willys by American Central Manufacturing are known as "ACM Type I" bodies.*

Fig 23 – *The more unitized and rounded floor bracing used on Ford-built GPW bodies and on ACM Type II bodies, which are also known as "composite" bodies.*

of an MB, whether or not the engine in any particular WWII jeep is an original, or a WWII vintage replacement engine for that matter. If you are interested in further decoding the casting codes, etc., reference books and websites can provide insight into these. (see appendix)

Frame

Willys MB and Ford GPW frames are easily distinguished from each other, and yet again are functionally interchangeable. The most obvious distinguishing feature is the front frame crossmember located beneath the grill and visible from the front of the vehicle. All Willys frames were built with a tubular front frame crossmember. 99% of all Ford GPWs were built using an open channel type front crossmember that resembled an inverted "U" in cross-section. The only exception to this is a very small number of very

early GPW's built on Willys style (tubular front crossmember) frames. These GPWs are very rare and rather collectible. (Fig 20, 21)

Other design differences exist between Willys and Ford frames. The shock absorber mounts are of different design. There are numerous lightening holes in the GPW frame that are not present on a Willys frame. Willys frame channels are less "boxed-in" than Ford's. There is a major difference in the design of the machine-gun pedestal mount between Willys and Ford and more; however, the front frame crossmember remains the most tell-tale and visible feature.

Body

There are six main assemblies comprising the entire body of the jeep: hood, grill, two fenders, windshield frame, and the "tub". The "tub" is the large main part of the body in which the seats are mounted. The tub extends from the firewall, just behind the engine, to the rear panel on which the spare tire bracket is mounted. Design differences exist between Willys and Ford fenders, grills, windshield frames, and hoods, but these differences are subtle. Differences between Willys and Ford manufactured tubs used on very early MBs and early MBs and GPWs are significant. As mentioned before, after 1943 both MBs and GPWs used identical ACM—built "composite" bodies.

The most apparent differences between early MB and early GPW tubs can

Fig 24 – The smooth, flat topped tool box lid characteristic of a Willys MB. Note the circular depression on the side of the tool box for the toolbox lock. This circular depression was used on all ACM built bodies (Type I and Type II).

Fig 25 – The embossed top of a Ford GPW tool box lid. Note the rectangular depression for the tool box lock. This rectangular depression is only found on Ford-built GPW bodies.

be found in the design of the floor bracing and toeboard braces. The early MB tub floor bracing is comprised of many individual angular parts and the early MB toeboard braces are simple triangular braces with five lightening holes in each. The floor bracing of the Ford-built bodies is a more-curved, unitized affair and Ford-built toeboard braces are again more curved with three lightening holes in each. (Fig. 22, 23)

What can confuse the jeep enthusiast when trying to identify a particular tub is that the ACM "composite" bodies use the same floor bracing and toeboard braces as the Ford-built tubs. In order to distinguish between a Ford-built tub and an ACM composite tub one must look beyond the floor and toeboard braces. In essence, the ACM composite tub is basically a Ford-built front half mated to a Willys style rear half, with the break positioned at the floor step area just ahead of the machine gun mount. The Willys body tubs have circular depressions for the toolbox locks to rest in whereas the Ford-built bodies have rectangular depressions for the toolbox locks. Because, the ACM composite body uses a Willys style rear section, the ACM composite body looks like a Ford-built body except that it has circular toolbox lock depressions. (Fig. 24, 25)

The items bolted to the tubs such as hood, fenders, toolbox lids, etc., are, as usual, fully interchangeable between Ford GPWs and Willys MBs, but are also fully distinguishable as to identity of manufacturer. An early Ford GPW would be supplied from the factory with a Ford-built tub and Ford-built pieces attached to it. A late-war Ford GPW with an ACM composite body would still have Ford-built items bolted to the ACM tub.

Likewise is true for Willys jeeps. After leaving the factory, parts were often swapped during wartime without regard for manufacturer and so it is not uncommon, nor is it unacceptable to see a

Fig 26 – The lighting system on a standardized WWII jeep. A) Blackout marker lights, B) service headlamps, C) blackout drive light.

"motorpool" style jeep sporting a mixture of Willys and Ford parts. A skillful vehicle judge can easily spot a Willys part mounted on a Ford jeep.

Electrical and Lighting

The standardized WWII jeep is equipped with a six-volt negative-ground electrical system. Power is supplied by an Auto-Lite GEG-5101D 40 amp generator and is regulated by an Auto-Lite VRY-4203A Current Voltage regulator. Some differences did

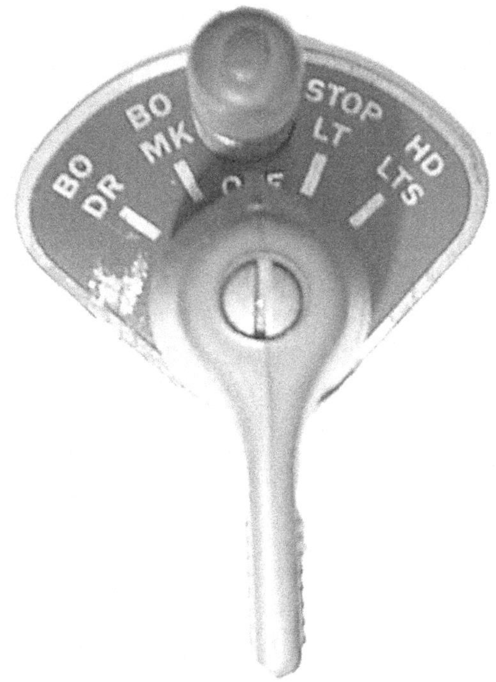

Fig 27 – Late-war rotary light switch which was easier for the GI to operate.

occur through the production history of the WWII jeeps. Very early MBs came with 25 amp generators and regulators and a small number of standardized WWII jeeps were equipped with a 12-volt system conversion to power radio sets.

The typical battery found in WWII jeeps was either an Auto-Lite TS-2-15 in MBs or a Willard SW-2-119 in GPWs. Both are three-cell external connector type batteries measuring 10in X 7in X 8 5/16in high.

The jeep's simple lighting system consists of two service headlamps, two blackout headlamps, one blackout driving light, service and blackout stop and tail lights, and two instrument panel lights. (Fig. 26) The lighting system is protected by a thermal circuit breaker mounted on the main light switch behind the dashboard. Two other circuit breakers mounted on the dashboard to firewall brace protect the horn and fuel gauge circuits.

Even though the jeep's electrical system is simple, understanding the operation of the jeeps single main light switch is a bit mysterious to the first-time driver. In order to understand the light control switch, the driver must realize that the jeep has four basic modes of lighting. On WWII jeeps built before June of 1944 the four modes were selected by use of a push-pull type switch with four "stops", after June 1944 a more easily understood rotary style selector switch with five positions was used. Both the push-pull and the rotary style switches had a thumb-lock mechanism to prevent the accidental illumination of lights during blackout conditions. (Fig. 27, 28)

Mode 1 (full in on push-pull or center "OFF" position on rotary switches) can best be described as "total blackout condition". In this mode, absolutely no lights illuminate on the jeeps at all, not even brake lights.

Mode 2 (out one stop on push-pull switches, first position to the left of center

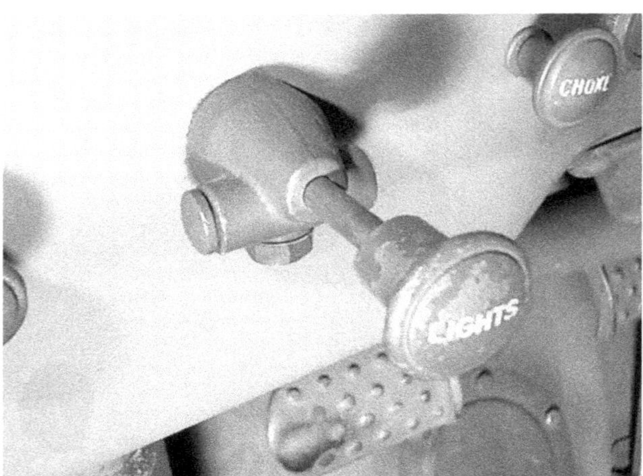

Fig 28 – *Push-pull light switch used on almost all WWII vehicles including jeeps.*

"BO MK" on rotary style switches) is best thought of as the "blackout driving mode". In this position the jeeps blackout marker lights are illuminated both front and rear and the blackout stoplights are functional. Also in this mode, the driver may elect to illuminate his left-fender mounted blackout drive light. The pre-June 1944 jeeps have a separate switch that is used to illuminate the blackout drive light. To illuminate the blackout drive light on later jeeps the rotary switch is turned to "BO DR" position, two stops to the left of center. This action requires the operator to depress the lockout control button.

Selecting Mode 3 requires that the lockout control button be depressed on both types of switches. With the lockout control button depressed the push pull switch can be pulled to the second stop, or the rotary switch can be rotated to the second stop to the right of center "HD LTS". This position illuminates the service headlamps, the service tail lamps and it activates the service stoplights. In other words, this is the normal nighttime lighting mode. In this position the dashboard panel lights can be illuminated using the separate "Panel Light" switch on the dash.

Mode 4 is selected by pulling the push-pull light switch fully out or rotating the rotary style switch to the first stop to the right of center "STOP LT". This mode is the normal daytime mode in which the service stoplight is the only illuminated light on the vehicle when the brakes are depressed.

It is important for the WWII jeep driver to remember to leave the light switch in Mode 4 position during daylight hours to be sure that the brake lights will function.

The dashboard instrument panel lights found on standardized WWII jeeps are highly shielded so as to only allow a very thin beam of light onto the instruments. The shielding "caps" are oftentimes modified by cutting away a portion of the metal caps to allow more light to escape and light the instruments more brightly. (Fig. 29)

The ignition switches found on WWII jeeps were a key type until the fall of 1942 at which point a change was made to a keyless "toggle" type switch. The starter switch on all WWII jeeps was a foot operated type mounted above and to the right of the accelerator pedal.

The wiring in the standardized WWII jeeps is composed of cloth-covered color-coded wire utilizing a combination of several different colors along with the incorporation of white "tracer" threads in the wire's cloth covering to identify each wire. For example, the wires feeding electrical power to the high beam service headlamps have two white tracer threads woven into a red cloth covering. The low-beam service headlamps are powered via wires having three white tracers in a black cloth covering. This system allows for easy tracing of wires from point to point.

In addition to the electrical delivery system described above the standardized WWII jeep has a system of grounding straps, shielding and capacitors that combine to form a radio noise suppression system. Grounding straps connecting the choke and throttle cables, the fuel line, the exhaust pipe, the hood, and numerous other components to ground work in con-

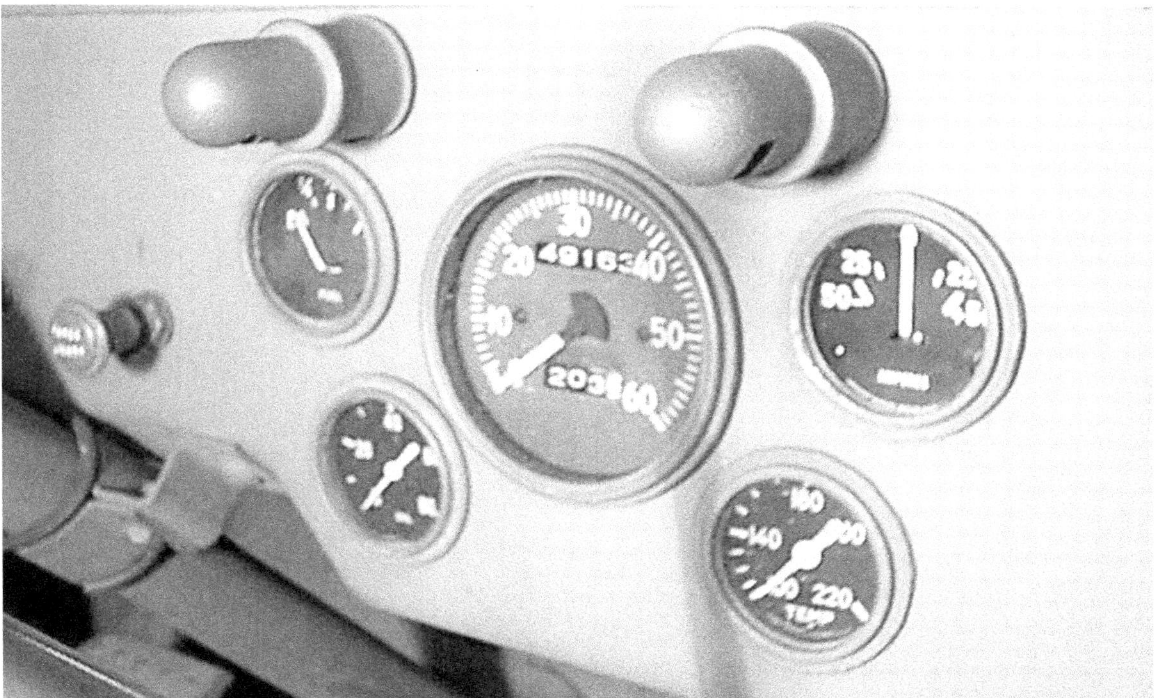

Fig 29 – *The bullet-shaped instrument panel lights are controlled by the panel light switch seen in the far left of the picture. The WWII speedometer has a trip-odometer.*

cert with wire shielding and capacitors to absorb and isolate radio frequency "noise" which might interfere with nearby radio communications or might disclose ones presence to enemy radio operators. Small capacitors are located in various locations throughout the jeep, and in most of the standardized WWII jeeps built, a bank of three large capacitors are located in a rectangular metal box mounted on the firewall under the dash board. This capacitor box is called a "Filterette" and was used for this purpose in many WWII vehicles. The radio noise suppression system on WWII jeeps was tested at the manufacturers facility and once found to be functioning properly, the jeep was marked with an "S" on its cowl (see Markings section). The Filterette was eliminated in late war jeeps and was replaced with the "Type II" suppression system which used more small capacitors in various locations. (Fig. 30,31)

Fuel System

The WWII jeep fuel system utilizes a fuel tank mounted in a floor sump under the driver seat. The tank has a capacity of 15 US gallons and is filled by lifting the cushion of the driver's seat to access the fill cap. Most fuel tanks on standardized WWII jeeps were equipped with a large-mouth fuel cap to facilitate filling from gas cans, but early Ford and Willys jeeps had smaller diameter filler necks and caps. The fuel is delivered by 5/16 inch steel fuel lines

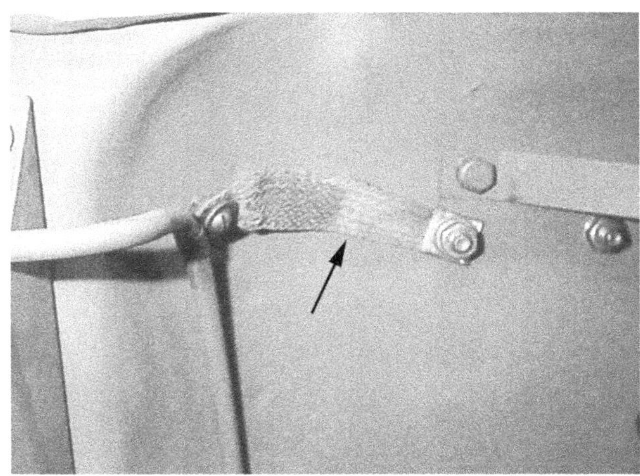

Fig 30 – *A bond strap connecting the fuel line to the firewall. This is one of many similar straps that are part of the jeep's radio noise suppression system.*

to a large strainer-type fuel filter mounted on the firewall directly ahead of the glove box. This strainer type fuel filter has a drain plug to drain off debris and water which might accumulate in the strainer bowl. (Fig. 32)

The fuel then is carried down the side of the inner fender, over to the engine and across the front of the engine to the fuel pump. The WWII jeep fuel pump is a mechanically operated diaphragm type pump with a sediment bowl on top and a hand operated primer lever mounted on the side. The sediment bowl on WWII jeep fuel pumps is plated steel. These steel sediment bowls were often replaced with civilian style glass bowls after WWII. (Fig. 33)

The primer lever on the fuel pump is used to prime the fuel system and deliver fuel to the carburetor before starting the jeep in cold conditions or in the event of fuel exhaustion. By manually operating the fuel pump primer lever, fuel from the tank can be drawn throughout the system filling all the fuel lines, the filter/strainer, the pump and the carburetor without having to wear down the battery by cranking the engine. This is a wonderful feature that was often lost after WWII when civilian owners replaced the original fuel pumps with civilian glass-bowled fuel pumps which did not have primer levers.

The carburetor on standardized WWII jeeps is a conventional downdraft single-barrel Carter WO-539S. Air is supplied to the carburetor by an Oakes brand oil-bath air cleaner that mounts on the right side of the firewall.

Fig 32 – The firewall-mounted fuel filter installed on the passenger side of the firewall under the hood on all but the latest WWII jeeps.

Fig 33 – The WWII jeep fuel pump has a metal sediment bowl and a hand-operated primer handle indicated by the arrow.

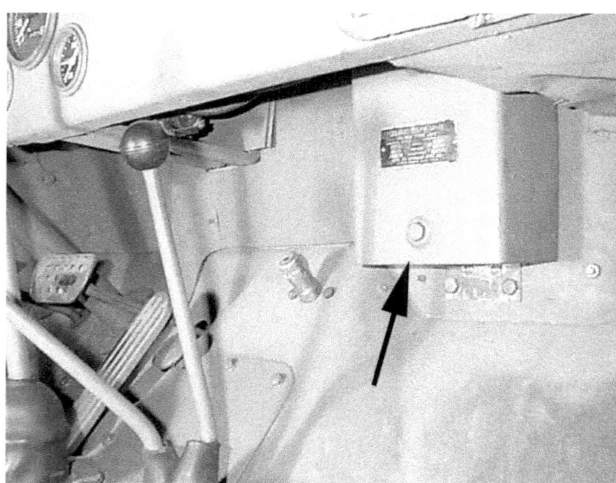

Fig 31 – The arrow identifies the Filterette mounted on the firewall under the dashboard.

Fig 34 – *AC "pancake type" air cleaner introduced with the production start in late 1941. Instructions placed on a small decal (black letters on red background). Those used on early GPWs are the only air cleaners that are "F" marked. (see section on "F" marks later in this chapter)*

Fig 35 – *Oakes "decal type" air cleaner introduced in early 1942. Instructions placed on a large decal (silver letters on black background).*

Fig 36 – *Oakes "plate type" air cleaner introduced in mid 1942. Instructions were embossed onto a steel plate which was attached by spot-welds.*

Fig 37 – *Oakes "standard type" air cleaner introduced in late 1942. Instructions were directly stamped in raised letters on the air cleaner case itself.*

Because the air cleaners on jeeps from 1941 through 1953 are functionally interchangeable and easily removed and swapped, early jeeps are often missing their original, correct air cleaners. Four styles of air cleaners were used during WWII jeep production.

Of the four styles used, the Oakes "standard type" is the most common WWII vintage air cleaner used on standardized jeeps during WWII. Types one, two and three were in use during the first year of jeep production which only accounts for about 30% of all WWII jeep production.

Wheels and Tires

WWII standardized jeeps were equipped with 6.00 X 16 non-directional tread (NDT) bias ply, tube-type tires. Several manufacturers including Firestone, Goodyear and others supplied these tires. Early GPW's normally were equipped with Ford-marked tires and later were supplied with Firestone tires. MBs generally were equipped with Goodyear tires. Once in service however, the tires were routinely replaced with other 6.00 X 16 NDTs with no regard to brand. Intermittent supply shortages during production may have also caused manufacturers to use alternative brands

Fig 38 – *6.00 X 16 NDT tires. The tread pattern on the left is a correct WWII style with pointed notches. The tread pattern on the right with rounded notches is commonly found on modern reproduction NDT tires.*

Fig 40 – *A complete MB rolling chassis.*

Fig 39 – *The standard WWII jeep combat wheel. The two-piece rim is held together with eight bolts – the heads of which are visible.*

wide drop-center solid disc wheels. (Solid disc wheels are confusing to identify -see appendix)

Power Train

The WWII jeep power train is a simple, sturdy design whereby power from the Go-Devil engine is transmitted to the wheels via a three-speed transmission coupled to a two-speed transfer case. The standardized WWII jeep uses a Warner T84J three speed transmission that incorporates a standard "H" shift Pattern. The shift pattern is displayed on a data plate found on the jeep's glovebox door. The transmission is synchronized from first to second to high gear. Switching back from high to second gear is also automatically synchronized, but, as is typical of trans-

from time to time. Very early MBs and GPWs were supplied with 6.00 X 16 tires with unusual tread designs such as the Firestone "ground-grip" tire used on early GPWs, but these types of tread were the exception and not the norm throughout the war. Two tread styles can be found in use during WWII (Fig 38). Tires with a "V" – shaped cut-out were commonly supplied with jeeps during the war, but rounded notch tires also made their way into service. The rounded notch design persisted after the war.(Fig. 38)

Two piece bolt-together steel rims called combat rims or combat wheels were supplied with all standardized WWII jeeps except for the very early Willys slat-grill MBs (before vehicle serial number MB120700). The slat Grill MBs were supplied with more conventional four inch

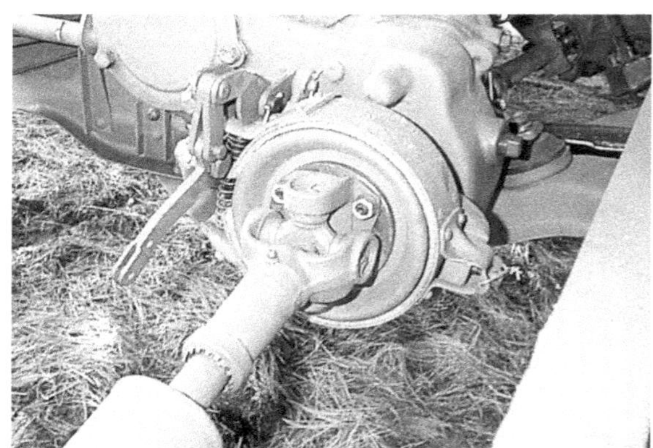

Fig 41 – *The external contracting band handbrake mounted on the rear output shaft of the jeep's transfer case. A leaking transfer case output shaft oil seal can quickly soak the brake band with oil rendering this brake useless.*

missions of its day, shifting from second into first requires double-clutching to synchronize the gears and prevent grinding.

The Spicer Model 18 transfer case used in WWII jeeps is a non-synchronized two-speed transfer case that allows the operator to select two or four wheel drive. High and low gear or "range" are permitted in four-wheel-drive, but an internal interlock only permits high range in two-wheel-drive. Operating the jeep in two-wheel-drive low range would deliver too much torque to the rear axle and could cause damage. In low range four-wheel-drive the torque is distributed more evenly between both the front and the rear axle helping to prevent driveline damage. Selection of high or low range and two or four wheel drive is accomplished by the use of two shift levers mounted on the transfer case. Again, the transfer case shift pattern is displayed on a data plate found on the jeep's glovebox door (see Figure 10).

The WWII jeep's handbrake acts upon the rear output shaft of the transfer case. Pulling the handbrake lever mounted in the middle of the dashboard tightens a brake band around a brake drum that is attached to the transfer case output shaft. This in turns stops movement of the rear driveshaft and (in theory!) stops the vehicle. The WWII jeep handbrake is a fickle affair that works well only if in good condition.

The front and rear axles are Spicer full-floating axles with a gear ratio of 4.88:1. The front axle has specially designed sealed spindle housings (steering knuckles) which house one of three types of constant velocity joints (Rzeppa, Bendix or Tracta). The axles are mounted on semi-elliptical leaf springs with the second leaf wrapped around the spring eye of the first (main) leaf. An additional spring assembly is found on the driver-side front axle on jeeps built after late 1942. This additional spring is called a torque reaction spring and was added to jeeps to help minimize

Fig 42 – *The torque reaction spring is mounted below the normal road spring on the driver side of the jeep. Its purpose is to stabilize the front axle in braking situations.*

front axle roll and subsequent adverse steering effects during hard braking. Many earlier 1942 jeeps that came from the factory without torque reaction springs had the torque reaction spring added as a field modification. (Fig. 42)

The jeeps service, or foot brake system is a hydraulic four-wheel single system type utilizing a single master cylinder and nine-inch brake drums on each wheel. In modern vehicles the brake pedal actually controls two separate subsystems which are jointly activated . This is done so that in case a major leak occurs in one system,

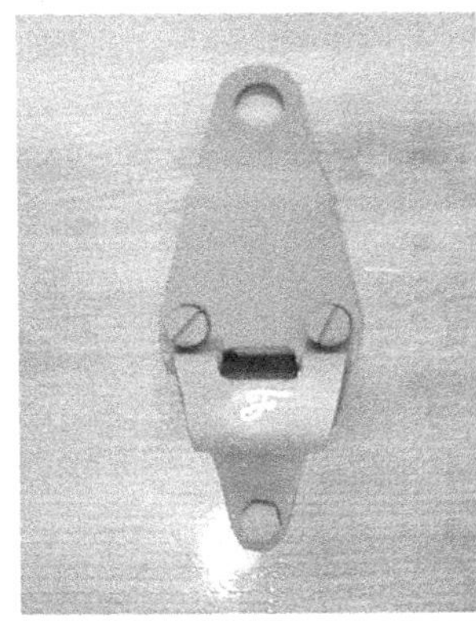
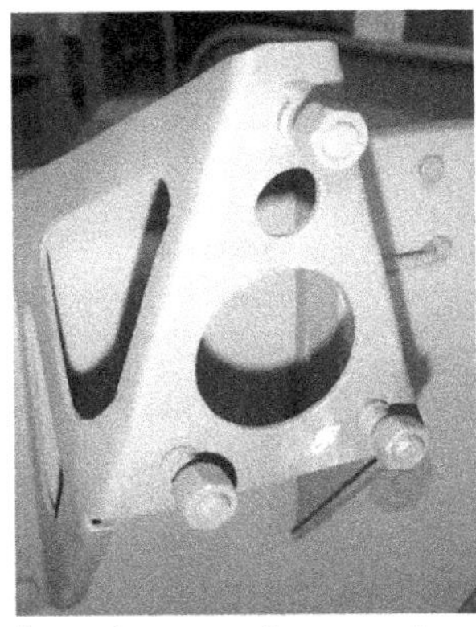

Fig 43 – *(left) Many Ford parts are stamped with an "F" such as this Ford GPW top-bow bracket. The "F" stamping has been highlighted with chalk in this image.*

Fig 44 – *(right) Another ubiquitous Ford "F" mark found on an early style three-bolt spare tire bracket from a GPW.*

the other will still function. This is not true with the WWII jeep's simple single system. A major loss of fluid or master cylinder malfunction will cause total loss of braking ability. The master cylinder is inspected and filled through an access hole in the floor on the driver side of the vehicle. The brake shoes must be manually adjusted as the linings wear.

Ford Marked Parts

Even though every individual part of a Willys built WWII jeep is perfectly inter-changeable with its Ford GPW counter-part, each part can be identified as either a Ford GPW or a Willys MB part. In fact, in many cases the Ford GPW part is actually marked with a Ford "F" of either block-style or script-style. (Fig. 43, 44)

These so called "F" marks can be found on almost every part of a Ford GPW right down to the bolt heads. Don't misinterpret this to mean that a proper Ford GPW must have ALL "F" marked parts however. Certain parts, such as the horn bracket for example, are not marked with an "F" but are still distinguishable from a Willys horn bracket by a slight difference in the fin-ished shape of the bracket. Furthermore, not every Ford GPW that left the Ford factories building them was equipped with every Ford-marked part imaginable.

In general, most of the parts on a GPW seem to have been "F" marked at one time or another during jeep production, but it seems that at any particular time one will find some non-"F" marked parts being used. This is probably due to changes in suppliers, different part production runs and other adaptations used to counteract shortages so common during wartime production.

Many internet websites (including the author's) offer images of "F" marked parts to help the collector/restorer identify their parts.

Accessories

The WWII jeep came from the factory with a substantial list of accessory items such as tools, jack, spare parts kit, hand crank, tire pump, etc. In addition to the factory supplied accessories many vehicular accessories were also added by the military before putting the jeep into service such as the axe and shovel (known as "pioneering

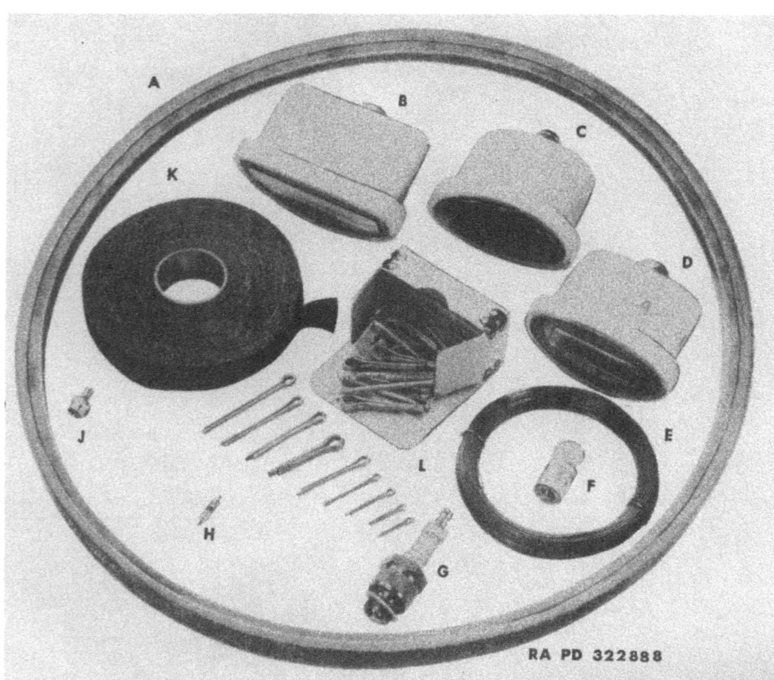

Vehicular Spare Parts

Bag, spare parts
Belt, fan [A]
Caps, tire valve (box of five) [J]
Cores, tire valve (box of five) [H]
Lamp, No. 63 [F]
Lamp unit, blackout stop [D]
Lamp unit, blackout tail [B]
Lamp unit, service tail & stop [C]
Pin, cotter, assorted (box of 75) [L]
Plug, spark [G]
Tape, friction (8oz roll) [K]
Tire, 6.00X16 mud & snow NDT
Tube, 6.00X16 heavy duty
Wheel, 16X400, combat
Wire, iron spool [E]

Fig 45 – *Vehicular Spare Parts*

tools") mounted on the driver side of the jeep. Further still, many specialized accessory items became available for jeeps as the war went on. These specialized accessories were added on an as-needed basis when the items were available such as the late-war winter enclosure or the front bumper mounted capstan winch.

The list of factory supplied accessories varies slightly with the date of delivery of WWII jeeps, but normally includes the following items listed below:

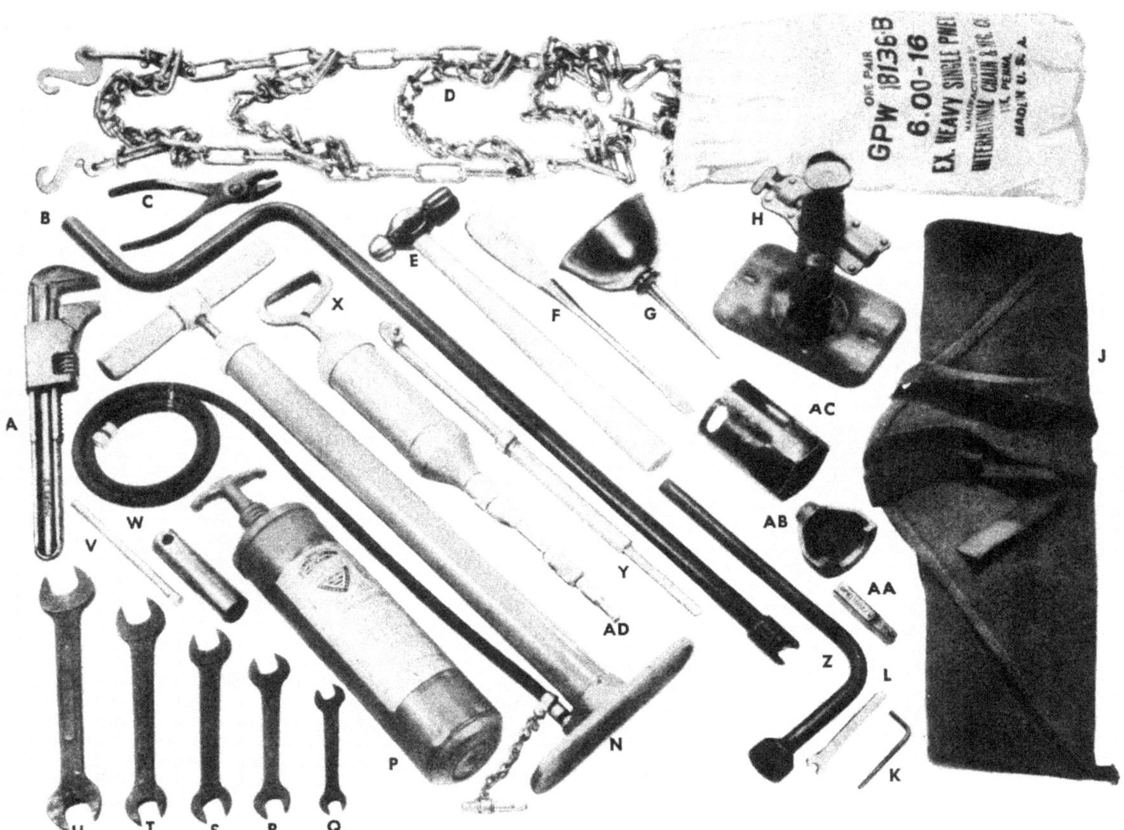

Fig 46 – *Vehicular Accessories*

Vehicular Accessories

Adapter, grease gun [AD]
Bag, tool [J]
Book, TM9-803
Chains, tire [D]
Cover, canvas headlight
Cover, canvas windshield
Crank, starting, engine [B]
Extinguisher, fire [P]
Gage, tire pressure [Y]
Guide, lubrication (War Dept. No. 501)
Gun, lubricating grease [X]
Hammer, ball peen, 16 oz. [E]
Handle, spark plug wrench [V]
Jack, screw, w/handle [H]

Oiler, can, ½ pt. [G]
Pliers, combination (6in.) [C]
Puller, wheel hub [AB]
Pump, tire w/air chuck [N]
Screwdriver, 6 in [F]
Tarpaulin, deck top
Wrench, adjustable, auto type (11 in.) [A]
Wrench, drain plug [AA]
Wrench, set of five, engineers (3/8" through 7/8") [U,T,S,R,Q]
Wrench, Bristol, fluted [K]
Wrench, brake bleeder [L]
Wrench, spark plug socket [W]
Wrench, wheel bearing nut [AC]
Wrench, lug nut [Z]

CHAPTER 2
Buying a WWII jeep

Okay, so you're considering taking the plunge and getting a real WWII jeep of your own. I think it's a great idea and I know you won't regret it, providing you actually get what you want to get. This requires that you know two things:

1. A basic knowledge of WWII jeeps (that's what chapter one was for).
2. A vision of what you want for your WWII jeep.

Reading chapter one and researching other jeep literature and websites will take care of number one above. To develop the vision in number two will require you to ask yourself a few questions.

- Do I want to restore this jeep myself, have it restored for me, or do I want it all-done-ready-to-go?

- Is this jeep for showing only? If so, what level of competitive showing? National contender, regional MV events, or local car shows only?

- Is this a museum quality vehicle or more of a "motorpool" level jeep? Do you care if every nut and bolt are perfect and correct?

- Is this jeep for use in reenacting?

- Is this jeep for local parades and occasional drives to the ice-cream shop only?

- Will I go trail riding in this jeep?

- How important is authenticity and originality to me?

- Will this jeep be driven over the road or trailered to events only?

- How much can I spend on this jeep?

- Do I have good storage space available for this jeep?

- Is this jeep simply an investment or part of a larger collection?

- Am I looking forward to tinkering on this vehicle or does the sight of a wrench frighten me?

I cannot answer these questions for you, but in this chapter I hope to be able

Fig 47 – A restored GPW for sale. Is it worth the money?

to help you match your personal jeep vision with an actual vehicle. Clearly a very wide range of jeep visions can exist, but let's narrow it down to two main types of WWII jeep visions: jeeps which are already restored and ready to go, and vehicles needing restoration.

Buying a Restored jeep

Caveat emptor! Buying a restored jeep is by far the riskiest way to get a jeep, but on the other hand it can be the most economical and quickest way to a jeep. What makes the difference is the buyer's understanding of WWII jeep details and

Fig 48 – Some of the regional classified ad periodicals available at the local newsstand.

restoration techniques. Most often, a restored WWII jeep is not being offered for sale by the restorer themselves, but instead by a private owner who may have purchased it from the restorer or who purchased it from another owner who purchased it from the restorer long ago. You get the picture. Asking the restorer to explain details seen on the vehicle is not likely to be a possibility. Couple this with the fact that there are no real "standards" for restoration. Most jeeps are restored by amateur restorers whose skills and knowledge of jeeps can range from high to low. One of the most beautifully restored GPWs I've ever seen (which placed nationally, by the way) was restored by an amateur from New Jersey with an eye for detail and a understanding of WWII jeep history and development. On the other hand, any backyard mechanic can get an old WWII jeep, cobble it together with cj2a parts and give it an olive drab paint job and call it "restored." This practice is perfectly legal, somewhat dishonest and very confusing to the buyer. The best way to be sure that the "restored" jeep you are looking at is authentic and correct is to learn what to look for and examine the vehicle closely. In fact, the cobbled together cj2a/WWII jeep from the backyard mechanic may be perfectly suitable for your purposes (your jeep vision) if all you intend to do is trail ride for example. The problem comes when the buyer selects this poorly restored vehicle with the intent of showing it and finds out the hard way that it is sub-par, especially if the buyer pays top price for this jeep.

The Impossible Triangle holds true in buying a WWII jeep: Cheap, Fast, Good. You may pick any two of the three. You can buy a good jeep cheap, but it won't happen fast. You can find a cheap jeep fast, but it won't be good. And so on…

Where to Look

Remember that finding a good jeep for a fair price doesn't happen fast. It takes time, money and effort to find the right vehicle. The first step might be to join the Military Vehicle Preservation Association (MVPA) by visiting their website at www. MVPA.org. Aside from many other member benefits, the MVPA provides members with two periodic publications, *Army Motors* and *Supply Line. Supply Line* has many classified ads for military jeeps both restored and unrestored. By reviewing these ads you may or may not find the jeep of your dreams, but you will get a feel for current market values and availability. Another periodical that lists restored WWII jeeps is *Military Vehicles Magazine* (www.militaryvehiclesmagazine.com). The collector car bible, *Hemmings Motor News* (www.hemmings.com), sometimes has restored WWII jeeps listed also. Local or regional automotive classified ad magazines sometimes offer up some interesting WWII jeeps. On-line classified ad venues such as CraigsList and Facebook Marketplace also offer restored and project jeeps for sale. The usual cautions apply when using these on-line services.

The internet offers several opportunities to find restored WWII jeeps. The obvious choices like www.ebay.com come

Fig 49 *– G503.com, a good place to look on-line for jeeps for sale as well as lots of WWII jeep information.*

to mind, but remember that as explained above, you, the buyer, **must** be able to examine the vehicle closely before the deal is done. Any restored WWII jeep sold as-is, where-is, and "you must buy it now" would send me running away. You have the money so you get to call the shots on this deal. If the seller is not amenable to an inspection prior to sale, let the vehicle go to someone else. Another jeep will surface eventually. Other websites such as www. g503.com have "jeep for sale" listings that offer a wide variety of jeeps. I have seen some excellent jeeps pass through www. g503.com's jeeps for sale ads. The trouble with the internet is, of course, that the competition for these jeeps is widespread and they can be located very far from home.

My gut feeling on the most reliable way to find a good restored jeep is to get con- nected with people who are involved with WWII jeeps in your area. One way to do this is by joining your nearest MVPA affili- ated Military Vehicle Club. In these clubs you will meet people who are connected to the jeep "network" and who may know of jeeps for sale in your area. Also, you should keep your eyes open at parades and car shows where WWII jeeps might turn up. If you see a WWII jeep, talk with the owner and let him or her know that you are in the market for one. I field these inquiries all the time and I have connected several people with jeeps myself over the years. By getting the buyer and the seller together I end up doing two people a favor at once. Visit nearby museums and if they have a WWII jeep on display ask the museum personnel for information about where and from whom the jeep was obtained. Many museums are surprisingly helpful

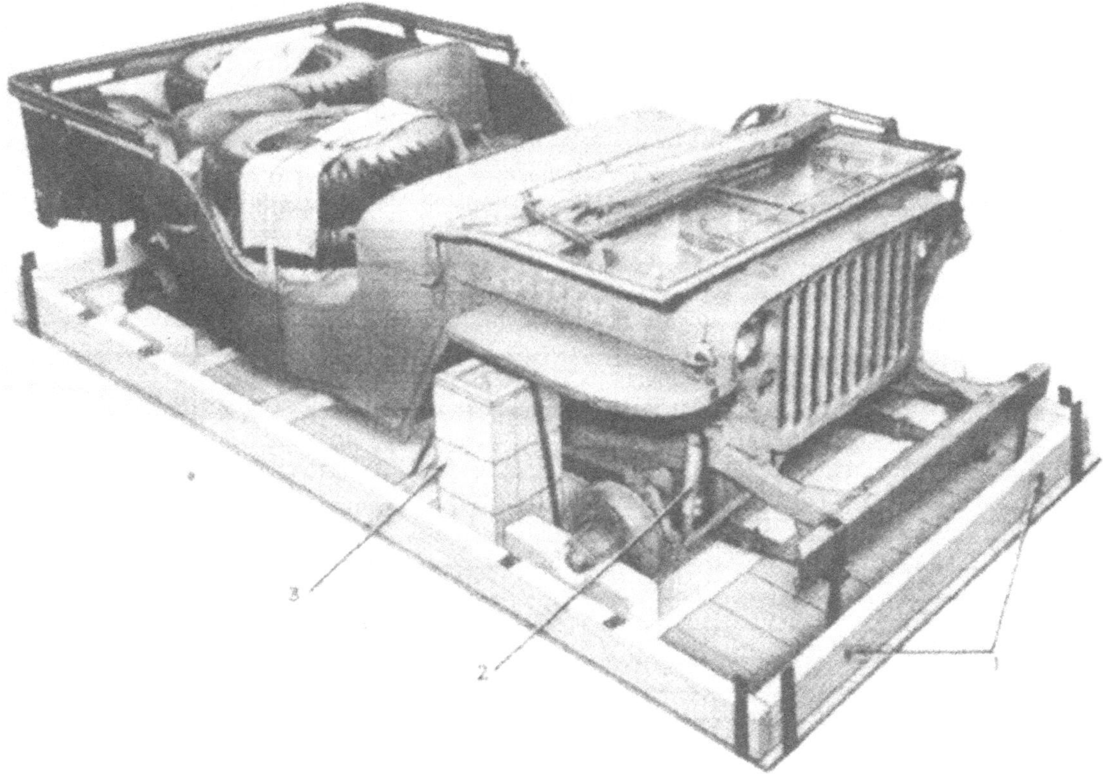

Fig 50 – *A WWII jeep-in-a-crate with the top and sides of the crate removed. Thousands of jeeps were crated and shipped overseas during the war, but no original crated jeeps exist today.*

in this regard and can provide you with valuable leads to WWII jeeps in your area. Working to establish a network of WWII jeep connections will eventually lead you to a jeep.

By the way, there are no WWII jeeps available at government auctions anywhere any more. Period. The last of the surplus WWII jeeps were probably sold off in the 1960s at the latest. Furthermore, the old, fabled jeep-in-a-crate for $50 does not exist and most likely never did. In the late 1940's and early 1950's, just after WWII when WWII jeeps were the most plentiful, and because of the law of supply and demand, were their cheapest, GI's with preferential buying privileges could buy a used WWII jeep for $500 and new ones for $750...not $50. $750 for a car in 1950 was not all that cheap - when adjusted for inflation it amounts to about

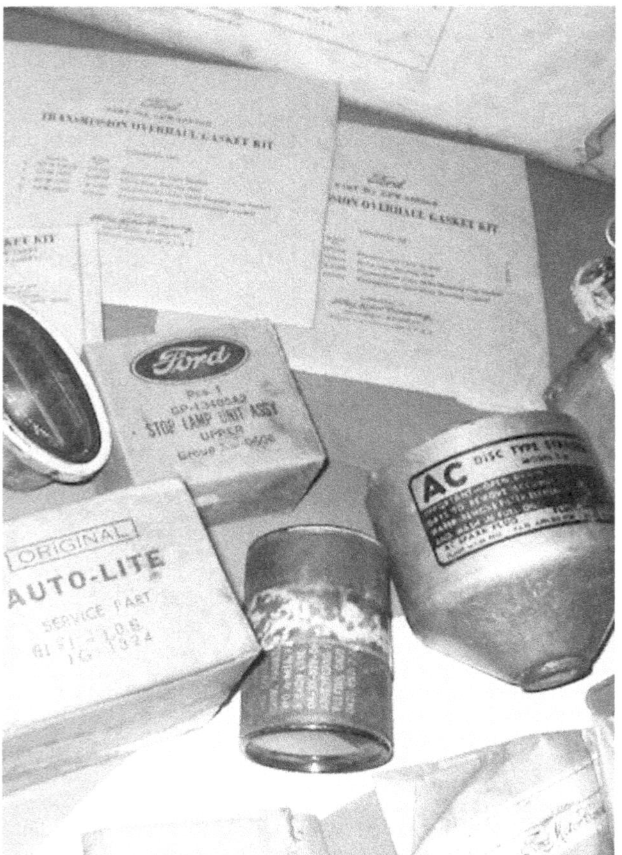

Fig 51 – *A collection of NOS WWII jeep parts and original packaging.*

$6680 today! The bottom line is the US Government is not going to be your source for a WWII jeep nowadays.

What to Look For

The act of restoring a WWII jeep is an exercise in compromise and decision making. The unrestored vehicle is completely disassembled and each and every part of that vehicle poses the restorer with a need for a decision. "Is this part acceptable to remain in the restored vehicle?" In a perfect world only those parts which are "good as new" would be good enough to stay in the project vehicle, but that still requires a decision on the part of the restorer. "IS this part good as new or is it not?" Furthermore, some parts are not available new, other parts are more valuable if they are not new reproductions but instead are 60 year old originals, still others are prohibitively expensive to replace unless necessary. Replacing every part with a new part is NOT the answer either. There are new parts (reproduction parts or "repro") and there are "new, old stock" (NOS) parts. NOS parts were made by the original part manufacturers during WWII as spare parts and were never used. A surprising amount of these NOS parts are still available today, but these command very high prices. It is generally accepted that installing an NOS part in a restored WWII jeep is no different than having an original part in place. On the contrary, replacing a worn or missing original part with a reproduction part (made recently by a third party manufacturer) is not considered to be an "original" piece and is therefore much less valuable. What does this mean? In a nutshell, the more repro parts used to restore a jeep, the less expensive the restored jeep should be. Are repro parts of lower quality than NOS parts? Not necessarily. Do repro parts look different from NOS parts? Not necessarily. Will a WWII jeep with NOS parts run better or look better than one with repro parts. Not necessarily. Will the WWII jeep restored with NOS parts cost more to restore than one restored with repro parts? Yes. This means that a jeep restored with repro parts should cost less than one restored with NOS parts.

Remember this! If your jeep vision is to own a national contender show jeep be careful to avoid jeeps restored using significant amounts of repro parts. If your jeep vision is to have an accurate looking, sound, and reliable restored WWII jeep, but showing the jeep at a high level of competition is not for you, then repro parts, used appropriately, should not be a concern.

Keep in mind that every recently restored jeep incorporates some reproduction parts. Canvas, rubber, glass, seals and gaskets, wiring, bearings, fluids, belts, hoses, paint and other components are routinely used modern day reproduction parts. These modern day repro parts are used because they are either safer to install (paint), safer to use in the vehicle than old dried out NOS originals (wiring), more reliable than old dried out NOS parts (seals and gaskets), or simply unavailable as NOS (canvas, rubber, glass). If a seller offers you a jeep with "no repro parts" ask him about the wiring or the canvas or the glass and see what he says.

In addition to the types of parts used in a jeep's restoration, the techniques applied in performing the restoration are critically important in deciding the value of the finished vehicle. The MVPA offers a *GPW Judging Standard and Restoration Guide*. If you are looking specifically for a restored GPW I would definitely urge you to buy this small book and use it to critique the vehicle you are considering. It specifies the details of a correctly restored Ford GPW includ-

Fig 52 – *Onlookers admire a jeep that has been beautifully restored by a hobbyist with an eye for detail and historical accuracy.*

When you inspect the jeep, bring along a notepad and a digital camera. Take some notes and LOTS of images of the jeep including details under the hood, etc. That way you can go home and review the pictures and notes with your reference books at your side. Don't trust all the details to memory... examining a picture in a quiet place may later reveal a problem that you may have overlooked during the initial inspection.

ing paint colors for components, types of fasteners used, and numerous details throughout the vehicle. If the vehicle you are examining is a Willys MB the MVPA unfortunately does not yet have the *MB Judging Standard and Restoration Guide* in publication, but being familiar with the GPW guide would give you a sense of the level of detail to look for in the MB. Many of the details are similar, but an MB is different enough from a GPW to prevent the guide from being interchangeable. Until the MB guide is available, you will need to rely on your own research and knowledge to evaluate the restored MB.

Another factor that plays into the value of the restored jeep is the overall thoroughness and quality of the restoration work done. A proper restoration requires a complete removal of ALL parts from the frame of the vehicle and the subsequent cleaning, inspection, repair or replacement of each individual part as the vehicle is reassembled. It is a time consuming process averaging probably 400 to 500 hours of labor—sometimes double that. This is why properly restored jeeps are expensive. (see appendix 6, 7)

Inspecting a Restored jeep

I've seen lots of "restored" jeeps in both my capacity as vehicle judge and simply as a restorer / enthusiast. Patterns have emerged as to the "corners most often cut" by amateur restorers in completing their jeep restoration project. Now, if you are searching for a national contender show jeep this short list of items to check by itself is very inadequate; likewise, if your jeep vision is of a good-running, accurate WWII jeep, these ten items to check can only help you eliminate the chaff from the grain and alert you to a vehicle that may be worth consideration or one to be avoided. Don't think of the Top-Ten list as a thorough evaluation technique, but instead consider it a first step in a restored jeep screening process.

Many amateur restorers do amazingly good work restoring their vehicles. These are the restorers who take the time to research the subject and apply historical authenticity to the decisions they make. Unfortunately, there is a group of "restorers" who seem to not even own a book let alone read it regarding the correct details of a WWII jeep. These "restorers" make their restoration decisions based on what is "cheaper", what "works" or what "looks right" based on very little understanding of the history, use, and development of the standardized WWII jeep. The items in the Top Ten List are ones that are either expensive to rectify or send up a red flag to me that this vehicle was restored without sufficient attention to detail.

Top-10 Checklist for Restored jeeps

- Starting and driving
- Serial numbers / data plate info / title
- Body condition
- Engine compartment
- Paint
- Electrical system/wiring
- Combat wheels
- Bumper gussets
- Dashboard / instruments / controls
- Markings

Number One—Starting and Driving

A pretty jeep that runs poorly is a constant

disappointment to its owner. The restored jeep should start easily and idle smoothly. There should be no trace of smoke from the exhaust. It should accelerate smoothly, shifting through all the gears without grinding or hesitation. The braking should be positive and straight. The steering should be tight (there is no hydraulic steering damper on a WWII jeep!) and the vehicle should be free of extraneous rattles and gear whine. Starting and driving is number one for a reason. If your jeep runs beautifully, it will be a pleasure to you and it is an indication of the level of quality of the restoration work done.

Serial Number/Data Plate Info

Numbers, numbers, numbers! Review the section from chapter one regarding serial numbers and be sure that the numbers on the restored jeep make sense. If, for example, the frame and engine numbers on a GPW do not match, then the vehicle is missing its original engine. This may not be a concern to you if you are not intending to show the jeep at high levels of competition, but it DOES affect the overall value of the restored jeep. All things being equal, a GPW with its matching numbers engine will command a higher price than the same GPW with a mis-matched GPW engine. A GPW with a Willys MB engine would command an even lower price and a GPW with a post-war CJ2a or 3a engine would be even more affordable. The serial numbers will tell you this information and can afford you some bargaining power with the seller!

Before you inspect the vehicle get the facts from your state's Department of Motor Vehicles regarding titling & registration of vehicles. Be certain that the restored jeep you are buying has the necessary title and paperwork to allow you to register it in your state.

Body Condition

Ideally, the restored jeep will have an original body in like-new condition. Skillful body workers can achieve this goal, but it is costly and time consuming. Many amateur restorers lack the skill of the experienced body worker and make up for that lack of skill with gallons of Bondo. Ahh…Bondo, also known as plastic body filler, or "jeep-in-a-can." Excessive or improper use of body filler leads to poor quality body repairs that can crack and blister over time. Using plastic body filler to fill rust holes is just plain wrong on a restored jeep. Rusted body panels should be either replaced with new panels or the rusted area should be cut away and new metal should be butt-welded into the cut-out. Plastic body filler can, in my opinion, be used sparingly on properly restored jeeps to fill grinder marks and such, and for minor leveling of patch panels just as body lead was used in the past. The plastic filler shouldn't ever exceed 1/16" thick and should not cover large areas of the body. Finding excessive plastic body filler in a jeep body sometimes takes very close inspection, sometimes it doesn't! Feel the lip around the rear wheel openings and along the bottom edge of the body below the axe and shovel groove and on the passenger side. This lip is a single thickness of 18 ga steel. If the "lip" feels thicker than a single thickness of sheet metal you can suspect plastic body filler use in these rust-prone areas. Noticeable plastic body filler use sharply reduces the

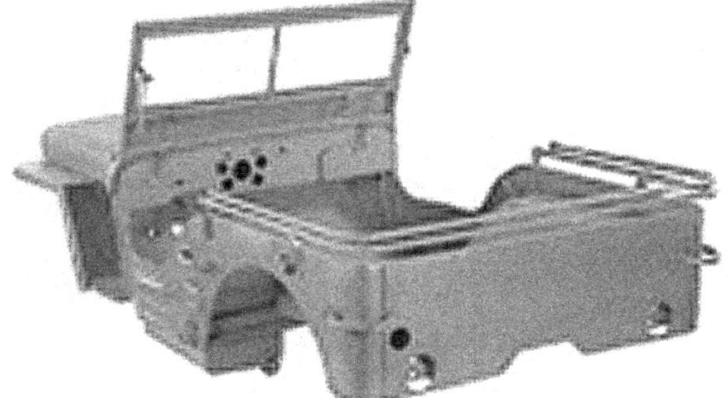

Fig 53 *– A steel reproduction body kit available from numerous suppliers worldwide.*

selling price of a restored jeep.

On the other end of the scale, restored jeeps are sometimes offered for sale which have brand-new reproduction steel bodies installed. The original bodies were either missing or deteriorated to the point that the restorer didn't have the time or skill to save the original body. I have already discussed the use of repro parts above and you must consider that an entire reproduction body is a major part of the jeep. Normally if two jeeps are otherwise the same, the one with the original body will command a substantially higher price, or to look at it from a different perspective, the one with the repro body will be considerably more affordable. Original body jeeps will hold their value better than ones with repro bodies as more and more repro-bodied jeeps come onto the market. I personally prefer an imperfect original body to a "perfect" repro body. For a competitive show jeep having an original body is virtually a "must"—for other uses, a repro-bodied jeep will be just fine.

Replacement bodies made of fiberglass have been available over the years. Yuk, don't go there.

Sometimes I see "restored" jeeps with post war cj2a hood and windshield installed. This is obviously wrong but easy to spot. The cj2a and cj3a hoods have the word "Willys" embossed on the sides. The cj2a windshield frame also has the word "Willys" embossed on it. A cj3a windshield frame is very different from a WWII style windshield frame. The WWII (and cj2a) windshield glass is in a separate frame that tips out at the bottom for ventilation; on a cj3a the glass is fixed in place and a small panel below the glass tips open for ventilation.

Engine Compartment

The engine compartment should be clean and properly painted. Check that the following items are present (or not present) and accounted for:

- WWII vintage generator (6 volt) NOT an alternator!
- Correct cloth-covered wiring - No plastic covered wire!
- WWII style (huge) voltage regulator on the right-hand fender
- Primer-handle fuel pump with metal strainer bowl
- No heater hoses (because there should be no heater!)
- Firewall mounted fuel filter (except on very late war jeeps) -No modern style in-line fuel filters visible
- Correct WWII air cleaner (see chapter one)
- Correct style horn
- No starter solenoid (jeep uses a foot-switch to actuate the starter)
- Correct T-84 transmission (not a later T-90)
- Correct side discharge exhaust
- Bonding straps (see chapter one)

These items are listed for two reasons. First of all they are easily ignored by the "restorer" because they are out of sight and therefore an easily rationalized corner to cut. Secondly, because they are expensive to do correctly during the restoration, they can be even more expensive to fix after the fact.

Paint

Arguments over the correct "shade" of OD paint that belongs on a WWII jeep have been raging on and on for years. One fact remains however: that all WWII jeeps were painted "lusterless olive drab". "Lusterless" means "without shine" or "flat". This is accepted and agreed upon: the paint on a WWII jeep should be olive green in color and flat, no shine, lusterless. Not semi-gloss or gloss, but flat!

A shiny vehicle in WWII was a recipe for disaster! The vehicles were painted lusterless olive drab to blend in with the environment as camouflage does. Shine

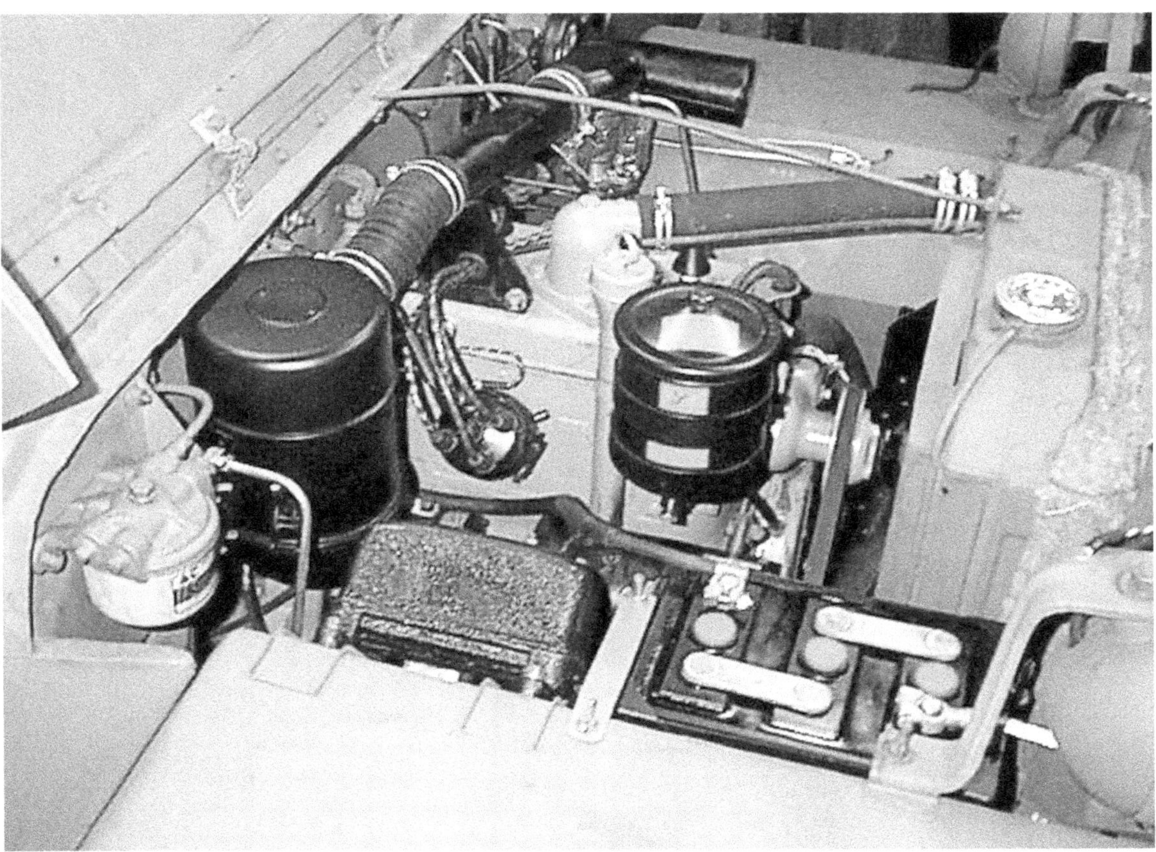

Fig 54 – *Engine compartment of a restored GPW.*

was dangerous. Some olive drab paint is greener than others, some is more tan or khaki than green—the hue can be argued, but the luster cannot, it must be flat. That said, many amateur "restorers" paint their jeeps with semi-gloss or gloss paint. This is not accurate, but is usually done because the restorer feels that the semi-gloss or gloss paint can be kept clean easier. I do not understand this thinking because to me a semi-gloss, or glossy standardized WWII jeep looks wrong and I really don't care if I can easily clean the fingerprints off a wrong looking jeep—it looks wrong with or without fingerprints to me!

The lusterless olive drab paint does in fact show fingerprints, oil spots and frequently handled areas such as grab handles tend to "shine-up" with use, but the overall end result is an accurate looking vehicle with a wonderful "patina" to it's finish. You don't think that fingerprints on

his jeep mattered for one minute to a GI in the hedgerows of Normandy, do you? Another advantage to the lusterless OD paint is the fact that it touches up very easily so small scratches and chips can be dealt with very effectively.

Properly repainting a shiny jeep is a very costly matter so consider the cost of repaint when making an offer on a shiny jeep.

Electrical System / Wiring

WWII jeeps were built over 60 years ago. The insulation on the electrical wiring originally installed at the time of manufacture is old and most likely dried out and prone to cracking. Old, dried out, cracked insulation leads to short circuits and potential fires which can make an awful mess out of your pride and joy. A good quality reproduction wiring harness is probably the only reproduction part that is a "must-have" on any good quality

Fig 55 – *Do you think these WWII GIs were concerned about fingerprints on the paint of these GPWs they were uncrating?*

restoration—for safety reasons. An NOS harness in excellent condition would be a better choice originality-wise, but these are very rare and the insulation on them is just as old and in my mind suspect of cracking—so repro it is. There are repro harnesses on the market that are essentially indistinguishable from the original harness and they are readily available. The use of a cobbled together, poorly made harness with plastic covered wire and crimped-on terminals is a sure sign of a compromised restoration.

Speaking of wire, the wire in a standardized WWII jeep is part of a six-volt electrical system, not a twelve-volt system. Many "restorers" convert their WWII jeeps to 12 volts to "improve performance" when in fact a six volt system in good original condition performs just fine. So why are so many jeeps converted to 12 volts? It is to overcome other problems that haven't

been properly addressed. For example, lets say that an original jeep's starter is showing wear and is in need of a rebuild. It cranks slowly on six volts, but it cranks just fine on 12 volts. Instead of fixing the starter (the real problem) some restorers convert the jeep's electrical system to 12 volts. The starter now cranks fine, but the problem has not been fixed. Oftentimes poor performance of six volt systems can be attributed to the use of undersized battery cables and corroded, dirty ground straps on the engine. Sometimes the reason the engine starts hard is because the fuel pump is defective, or maybe the engine needs a tune-up. In any event, converting to twelve volts often makes the symptoms (hard starting for example) go away, but it does not "fix" the problem nor is it authentic or necessary. I have started WWII jeeps with six volt systems in the dead of winter in Maine with great success. Converting a restored WWII jeep to twelve volts is not the answer it is a work-around and is cause for a reduction in value of the restored jeep.

Combat Wheels

This one is easy. Every standardized WWII jeep except for very early Slat Grill Willys MBs need to have five combat wheels installed. Four on the ground and one on the spare. Original combat wheels are prone to serious rust, warpage, cracks, and lug-nut-hole damage and in the past rounding up a good set of five combat wheel involved some scrambling around, wheeling and dealing and usually lots of cash. Today reproduction combat wheels are readily available and their price is slowly but surely dropping down into the realm of reality. They are still pricey averaging $150 to $200 per wheel depending on supplier, etc. so pay attention to the vehicle you are inspecting. If it lacks combat wheels or if they are in poor condition expect to pay at about $1000 + shipping + painting + installation costs to replace all five—ouch!.

Bumper Gussets

The front bumper gussets on standardized WWII jeeps are oftentimes damaged by years of abuse. Many WWII jeeps saw service after the war on farms, as snowplow vehicles, and in the woods. Consequently the front bumper and the gussets used to attach the front bumper to the frame are typically bent, cracked, welded-over or just plain gone. In inspecting a restored WWII jeep the front bumper gusset area deserves a close look. The original gussets on the WWII jeep were stamped steel roughly triangular braces that were riveted to the front frame rails. The bumper itself was bolted to the gussets using four long 5/16" bolts. Check the restored jeep's gussets to see how they are attached to the frame rails. Top-quality show jeeps must have the gussets riveted to the frame rails. Re-

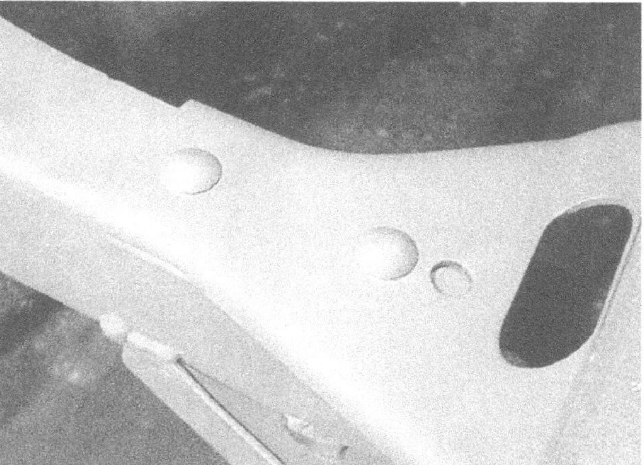

Fig 56 – Front bumper gussets are held to the frame with both rivets and welds.

placing rivets is difficult and corners are often cut in this area. Many times restorers bolt replacement gussets to the frame rails. Structurally, using bolts is fine, but it is not historically accurate and would be reason for a reduction in the value of the restored jeep.

I have compromised in this area myself by using button-head cap screws to simulate rivets when attaching replacement gussets to a frame. Button-head cap screws are better than plain old bolts, but not as accurate as actual rivets. The top, or visible side of the gusset shows the button-head filled with weld to simulate a rivet head, but by feeling inside the frame channel an inspector can feel the nut and lockwasher on the opposite end of the button-head cap screw (visit the author's website for details).

Dashboard / Instruments / Controls

Another area of concern on a restored WWII jeep is the dashboard. In general the dashboard should obviously have no extraneous holes drilled it and should have the proper switches and controls in their correct locations. Beyond these basics, the potential buyer should check to see that the gauges are of the correct type and vintage, especially the temperature

Fig 57 – A WWII jeep speedometer. A few different manufacturers and styles exist, but they all have the trip meter. Resetting the trip meter was accomplished via a knob on the back of the speedometer case.

gauge - whereas the temperature gauge is often missing / damaged / inoperable / or incorrect. NOS temperature gauges sell for about $250, so be sure of what is installed in the jeep before buying. The other expensive and difficult to find "gauge" is the speedometer.

Correct WWII jeep speedometers actually have a trip meter in addition to the usual odometer. The trip meter is reset by turning a knob mounted on the back of the speedometer. This involves reaching up under the dashboard and feeling around for the knob. Test the reset feature by turning the knob. No chrome bezels should be visible as this is a sure sign of an incorrect gauge. (Remember, nothing shiny on a WWII jeep, ok?) Check under the dashboard to verify that a filterette is in place except in very late-war jeeps utilizing the type 2 radio noise suppression system (see chapter one). While you are in the neighborhood, test the horn because the horn wire contact system in the steering column is prone to problems.

Markings

The markings on a WWII jeep are listed here not because they are an expensive item, but rather they can give a sense as to how concerned the restorer was with historical accuracy in details. You should look at both what the markings say and how they are applied.

First of all, the markings on a WWII jeep were all applied using paint during WWII, never vinyl stick-on numerals, etc. Blue-drab paint is used for the registration numbers and flat white paint for unit markings, stars, etc. Sometimes the registration number may be displayed in flat white paint if the vehicle is made to represent a jeep that has undergone a motorpool re-paint or is a very late-war vintage. Vinyl stick-on numerals are just plain wrong on a restored WWII jeep and indicate to me that the restorer was not concerned with accuracy, but instead based his decisions on looks or ease of application.

The second concern regarding markings is what they say. All standardized WWII jeeps built after the Willys Slat Grills of late 1941 should have a registration number that starts with "20". I have seen "restored" jeeps with registration numbers that were simply random numbers assigned by the restorer, vehicle serial numbers, the restorer's service ID number, even telephone numbers have been applied to the hood! This is not accurate! While a vehicle's original registration number may be lost over the years, it IS possible to determine an approximate possible registration number for any WWII jeep. All it takes is a bit of research in a few reference books on the restorer's part.

Review the section on markings in chapter one when examining a restored jeep with intent to purchase. The markings on a jeep are not a major part of the restoration, but they can give insight into the restorers commitment to accuracy.

What Will It Cost?

I am treading in dangerous areas with this topic, but it is a topic that needs to be addressed and after all, *someone's got to do it!*

Prices on restored jeeps vary widely with location, quality of the restoration, completeness of the vehicle, age of the restoration, style of WWII jeep and condition of the vehicle. Recent listings (2004) in *Supply Line* magazine have ranged from $4000 to $20,000 for WWII 1/4 ton jeeps listed as "restored". As the car ads always say—"your mileage will vary". We all know of people who have happened upon the deal of their lifetime with a good jeep cheap. We also know of folks who overpaid for jeeps by huge amounts. In this section please realize that I am speaking in general and on average. Your area may have traditionally higher or lower prices due to variations in supply and demand, but these figures are meant to be a guideline, not an absolute reference.

Top quality restorations probably average between $15,000 to $20,000 or more for 100% complete vehicle in factory-fresh condition. More collectible styles such as very early Willys Slat Grill or early Ford Script jeeps tend to command higher prices than later-war composite bodied MBs and GPWs. These top quality jeeps should pass the Top Ten list with flying colors and have a full complement of factory-supplied accessories. The use of major reproduction parts such as body tubs, frames, etc. is not expected at this level of restoration.

Good running complete restorations that show wear and have minor cosmetic problems that can be easily remedied generally run from $8000 to $14,000 depending on the amount of road grime and general wear apparent on the vehicle.

Fig 58 – A nice 1942 script GPW restoration candidate vehicle. This vehicle was virtually 100% complete, but not running. It sold for about $5000.

These vehicles should also pass the Top Ten list quite readily, but are not factory-fresh looking any longer. A fresh, clean restoration that uses major amounts of reproduction parts would also fall into this description and price range.

Incomplete restorations or restorations that have two or more areas of concern listed in the Top Ten list can be found for between $5000 to $8000. These jeeps will need additional investment of potentially thousands of dollars to bring them up to the level of the top quality factory-fresh restorations, but they may be excellent parade, reenactor, trail riding jeeps as-is.

WWII jeeps with serious defects or showing very poor restoration techniques or quality are normally available for $3500 to $5000. Generally speaking, a $3500 "restored" jeep will need some major work and cash to make it a reliable and accurate looking WWII parade or reenactor jeep if it is possible at all. Buying a very poorly "restored" $3500 jeep with the intent of fixing it up may be less economical than buying an unrestored jeep and starting from scratch. Oftentimes undoing the damage done by previous owners involves a significant effort and expense.

Buying a Jeep to Restore

Restoring your own WWII jeep is the surest way to control the quality of the finished vehicle. Whether you do all of the actual restoration work yourself, hire all the work out or some combination of these two methods, taking an active role in the restoration allows you to have a finished vehicle with little or no "surprises". Buying an unrestored vehicle and hiring out the complete restoration of the vehicle is the most expensive route to getting a WWII jeep. Buying an already restored vehicle is almost always more affordable, but as described above, it involves certain risks and uncertainties. Buying an unrestored jeep and doing the restoration work yourself can be the most affordable way to a restored WWII jeep depending on how much needs to be spent on up-front costs such as tools, storage areas, workshops space, etc. If you enjoy working with cars and trucks and find satisfaction in scraping off crud and sandblasting away rust and grime, then restoring your own jeep can be a very satisfying and rewarding process. It takes time, but for some hobbyists it is considered time well spent.

Whether you are doing the restoration work yourself or hiring out the complete restoration, finding a good candidate vehicle for restoration can make a big difference in the cost and the final product. Some hobbyist/restorers take pride in tackling the restoration of a vehicle that would be considered scrap by any sane person. I have seen some absolutely amazing transformations from what began as rusted out junk and ended up as beautiful finished vehicles. Most restorers however feel that the better the candidate vehicle is to begin with, the better the final product will be. This begs the question: "What is a 'better' candidate vehicle?" (I feel another Top Ten list coming on!) The fact remains that before we can evaluate a candidate vehicle we first must find one.

Where to Look

The suggestions offered in the previous section about where to find a restored WWII jeep also hold true for finding an unrestored candidate vehicle. The national military vehicle (MV) magazines and websites that list restored jeeps also have unrestored jeeps for sale. Some excellent candidate vehicles have been sold on the "for sale" message boards at www.g503.com for example. Local or regional automotive classified ad magazines again are sources for candidate vehicles.

One word of caution regarding the local classified ad magazines though: you need to look over any jeep that is listed in person. Many of the individuals listing old jeeps for sale in these local and regional classified ad magazines are unaware of what vehicle they actually have. The words "1946 Willys jeep for sale" in one of these ads does not necessarily mean that the vehicle is in fact a 1946 Willys jeep. I have responded to dozens of these ads and have found that the ad stating "1946 Willys jeep for sale" has in fact been everything from a 1942 Ford Script GPW, to 1944 Willys MB to 1948 Willys cj2a, to 1952 Willys M38, to 1956 M38A1 to a 1960 cj5. I kid you not! To the average person every old jeep is the same and is probably a 1946 Willys jeep. You can politely ask a few questions on the phone "how many slots are in the grill?" (7 slots = civilian, 9 slots = WWII) "Does it have a tailgate or glove box?", but my recommendation to you is to go and see

it in person. That is the only way to know for sure what is in fact for sale.

Another thing to keep in mind when looking for a candidate vehicle is the value of a parts vehicle. Let's say that you are looking to restore a mid-war Willys MB and you find one that is in very, very poor condition. Rather than passing completely on the vehicle, you might consider buying it anyhow, but continue searching. In time you will find a better candidate MB and you can use the one in poor condition as a parts vehicle. A parts vehicle is a wonderful thing. It can offer up both major and minor parts and it can be used as a reference to answer such questions as "Where does this clip go?" or "Does this wire pass inside or outside of that gusset?", too. I can honestly say that I have never lost money buying a parts vehicle. More often than not I will purchase the skeletal remains of a WWII

Fig 59 – Another 1942 Ford GPW restoration candidate vehicle peeks out from a tool shed.

jeep for $200, remove a dozen or so good parts and then sell the carcass for $200 to someone who does the same thing all over again, I suspect.

I said in the previous section that my gut feeling on the most reliable way to find a good restored jeep is to get connected with people who are involved with WWII jeeps in your area. This also holds true for unrestored vehicles, too. Review the comments from the previous section and start beating the bushes.

One last method for locating unrestored candidate jeeps is to keep your "jeep radar" on as you travel. Drive the back roads and look behind barns, sheds and in junk-filled lots. I have to admit that this method involves luck and sharp eyes, but I have found a few jeeps and one Bantam jeep trailer this way. Not all were for sale, but some were and I have also gotten a couple of parts vehicles by using "jeep radar". It's just another aspect of this wide and varied hobby (!).

What to Look For

Once you have located a WWII jeep in need of restoration you need to evaluate the vehicle to determine if it is a good candidate for restoration or not.

Sixty years ago the standardized WWII jeeps left Willys and Ford's factories in perfect condition and then the German and Japanese military did their best to destroy them. What the Axis powers failed to accomplish in this regard during the war, mother nature and man worked together to complete in the years since. The end result is that most unrestored WWII jeeps today are in pretty sad shape. The average person recognizes a 1953 Buick Sedan even in poor condition as a potentially valuable antique vehicle that probably should not be abused or destroyed. That same person sees a 1944 Willys MB as 'just an old jeep" and a potential driveway plower or sawmill power plant. The antique value is often overlooked and the "old jeep" is often abused or destroyed. Ahh, the poor jeep, a victim of its own versatility! Few jeeps were given graceful retirements, but instead were pressed into service long beyond their normal lifespan plowing snow, pulling stumps and towing hay wagons. When their original engines died, they were discarded and other replacement engines were fitted in place. When the two halves of the combat wheels rusted together, the assembly was tossed and any-old-wheel-that-fit was installed. A dozen or so different turn signals, rear view mirrors, flashing lights, canvas doors, plywood roofs, grab handles, tow bars, snow plows, trailer hitches, heaters and bucket seats were installed , then removed and installed again over the years. The body design is prone to rust in the first place, but filling the body tub with soggy leaves and leaving it parked outdoors for twenty years accelerated the rust problem to an extreme level.

What the restorer is left to contend with is a WWII jeep that is missing most of its original bolt-on parts, has the wrong engine installed, and has no combat wheels whatsoever. It has about two million holes drilled in the body and is rusted beyond belief. Ouch! On occasion a WWII jeep surfaces that is actually whole and complete and does not show all these symptoms, but it is rare.

In the previous section I offered up a Top Ten list for restored jeeps to be used as a tool for screening potential restored jeeps. A Top Ten list for screening unrestored jeeps may be useful, too. Keep in mind that the Top Ten list is not an exhaustive evaluation technique, but instead is meant to be a tool for initial screening of a potential restoration candidate jeep.

Top-10 Checklist for Unrestored jeeps

- Serial numbers / data plate info
- Frame
- Engine & Engine compartment
- Transmission / drive train
- Sheet metal
- Bumper gussets
- Combat wheels
- Dashboard / instruments / controls
- Miscellaneous bolt-ons
- Vehicle History

Serial Numbers/Data Plate Info/Title

Again I recommend that you review the section from chapter one regarding serial numbers and be sure that the numbers on the restored jeep make sense. If your goal is a national show contender these numbers are of critical importance. If showing the jeep at a high level of competition does not interest you, then the match between body/frame/engine numbers is less important, but it can influence the selling price of the unrestored jeep and the appraised value of the finished vehicle.

Different states have different requirements for titling and registering a vehicle. Before you inspect the vehicle get the facts from your state's Department of Motor Vehicles regarding titling and registration of vehicles. Look over the paperwork on the unrestored before buying it.

Frame

The frame is the foundation of the jeep vehicle. A sound foundation is critical for a solid restoration. While reproduction frames are now available, at about $900 and a couple hundred pounds they are costly to purchase and ship. A restorable vehicle with a solid, straight frame is most likely a better way to go. The front bumper gussets and rear crossmember are often damaged on unrestored vehicles, but both of these problem

Fig 60 – Under the hood of an unrestored MB. This vehicle was running, but many of the expensive under-hood components were missing.

GPW-195611
FORD ENGINE NUMBER
STAMPED
(GPW 195611) Note W shape
Boss under head, Forward of the Oil Tube
Check here for cracks
CASTING DATE C29 41
(Date) March29 '44
Right side
Ford "F"
FORD PART NUMBER
GPW-6015
Right side
Jon Rogers Pic

areas are repairable. A frame with serious rust, misalignment or cracking presents the restorer with some major challenges. Rusted, bent, cracked frames can be fixed, but it often involves specialized tools and skills. A solid, straight, original frame simplifies a restoration. The availability of repro frames has been spotty in the past and I have not used them nor have I seen them being used. Nonetheless, a restoration candidate with an unusable frame would certainly sell for a lot less than a similar vehicle with a solid frame.

Engine and Engine Compartment

The restoration candidate vehicle ideally would have its original engine installed (or included with the vehicle in some way). Check the engine numbers to verify that the engine under the hood is in fact the correct WWII MB or GPW engine. A restoration candidate vehicle with a post-war engine in place will sell for much less money. While you are under the hood note if some of the higher-priced items are present such as:

- Radiator ($250)
- Generator ($150)
- Starter ($200)
- Voltage regulator ($100-$250)
- Air cleaner ($80-$150)
- Firewall mounted fuel filter ($50)
- Swing-up headlamps ($100?)
- Correct cylinder head ($150)

(Notice that the short list above adds up to over $1200! The stuff under the hood is valuable!)

If the engine starts and runs that is great! Listen for unusual clatter or rattles from deep inside the motor. Look at the exhaust to see if it is blowing steam (cracked block and/or bad cylinder head or

Fig 61 – (left-hand page) Side view of a GPW block showing the area around the distributor boss where freeze-related cracking often occurs.

head gasket) or blue smoke (excessively worn cylinders and rings?) Look at the oil on the dipstick. If it is creamy brown there is water in the oil, probably from the cooling system (cracked block?), Does the oil smell of gasoline? (Fuel pump leaking into crankcase perhaps?) If possible test the compression on each cylinder. The compression test can tell a lot about the condition of the engine.

More often than not, the unrestored jeep is offered with a non-running engine. This is more of an unknown, but there are still things that can be checked. First look at the oil on the dipstick as described above. If there is no oil on the dipstick—why not? Ask the seller.

If the unrestored jeep is found in an area with freezing temperatures in wintertime, check the radiator to see that it is filled with antifreeze protected coolant (telltale green color and sweet smell of antifreeze). If the radiator is empty, then one of two things may have happened. The owner may have drained the coolant out of the block and radiator at some point in the past—this is probably ok. But why did he do it?—ask!. The other possibility is that the previous owner filled the radiator and block with plain water and forgot it there through the winter. The water froze, expanded and split the engine block and in the spring the water drained out of the block through the crack as it thawed—this is definitely bad. The most common place for cracks of this kind are in the engine water jacket around the distributor shaft opening. Check to see if this area exhibits telltale rust stains or obvious repairs of cracks from previous winters.

Try turning the crankshaft by hand. A person can turn the crankshaft in a healthy engine by applying pressure to the fan belt and pulling on one of the fan blades. If the crankshaft absolutely will not turn the engine is seized. If it seized from simply sitting for a long time a normal engine rebuild will usually correct this without much additional fuss. If the engine seized due to lubrication oil exhaustion, a spun crankshaft bearing, or worse a broken crank or connecting rod, the repair costs can be high. If it is seized, only disassembly and inspection will tell why.

A seized, cracked engine is essentially junk. Now, I know that cracks can be repaired and damage can be fixed, but the machine-shop costs can pile up real fast. A running, healthy engine is a lot simpler to rebuild with potentially fewer nasty surprises.

Transmission and Drive Train

Many unrestored WWII jeeps that have served time on a farm or in the woods have had their original transmissions "updated" with the more robust T-90 transmission that was standard in early post-war civilian jeeps (cj2a, cj3a, cj3b, M38 and cj5). The T-90 transmission can be made to fit into a WWII jeep but it isn't a clean installation. The floorboards need to be cut away a bit and the center frame crossmember needs to be butchered. The driveshafts are also swapped or modified. All in all the conversion from the original T-84 to the T-90 is altogether ugly and hard to undo. Be sure that the candidate vehicle has a T-84 transmission installed. The T-84 transmission is marked on its case but more obviously it is a flat-topped transmission whereas the T-90's top cover is elevated and more complex looking. Rebuilding your T-84 transmission is not all that difficult. Finding a new T-84 to replace a poorly installed T-90 can be problematic.

Sheet Metal

Here is where you can learn a lot about

Fig 62 – Rusted-out axe and shovel groove area. This area is one of several rust-prone spots on a WWII jeep body including the tool box bottoms, the floor support channels, and the front fender step.

rust. More than you want to know in fact…The sheet metal (body tub, fenders, hood, grill and windshield frame) can all be replaced as a unit for about $2400 plus shipping, but as discussed earlier, a restored vehicle with an original body will appraise for a higher value. Consequently, the restoration candidate vehicle with the repairable body is likely to cost more, too. Individual repair panels are available from many suppliers, so repairs, even to very rusty or damaged body parts, are possible. Be careful to look past repairs already made to the body by previous owners. Patches held on with pop-rivets and coated with Bondo (remember jeep-in-a-can?) are essentially worthless and will need to be removed and the underlying panel will need to be fixed correctly.

Don't pay extra for poor quality repairs that have already been done. For the most part the unmolested, albeit rusty and damaged, jeep body is preferable to the jeep body that has gallons of bondo and six layers of house paint on it hiding potentially serious problems. You know what is said—better the devil you know than the devil you don't!

Bumper Gussets

The front bumper gussets on an unrestored jeep are often in very poor condition. Reproduction front bumper gussets are readily available and can be installed as part of a restoration, but I suggest you look over the section on bumper gussets on a restored jeep. Properly replacing front bumper gussets using original style rivets requires specialized skills and tools. Compromising by using bolts or button-head cap screws is possible, but leads to a restoration with a somewhat lower value. How much lower? That is hard to say, but given the choice between two identical vehicles to restore I would pay more for the one with undamaged front bumper gussets.

Combat Wheels

A restoration candidate vehicle with five good combat wheels is automatically worth $750 to $1000 more than one missing all its combat wheels. Rusted, bent, cracked combat wheels are unsafe and worthless.

Dashboard/Instruments/Controls

Original instruments, in particular an original working temperature gauge, can add a few hundred dollars to the value of an unrestored vehicle. Be sure the vehicle has an original WWII speedometer—the one with the trip meter! Check under the dash for a Filterette (see chapter one) and if the vehicle is an early GPW look to see that it has the early stamped metal choke and throttle control knobs, these are very hard to find. (I paid $90 for an NOS stamped metal choke control for my latest GPW restoration—and I was lucky to find one at all.) The steering wheel should be in good condition without cracks or bends, too.

Miscellaneous Bolt-on Items

The bolt-on items that are so often missing from WWII jeeps are all readily available as reproduction pieces, but the overall cost of these items adds up quickly. A "stripped" jeep can require a substantial amount of cash to replace its missing bolt-on items. Consider this short list:

Axe bracket	$20
Bumperettes	$60
Grab handles	$60
Top bows and brackets	$300
Rear seat frame	$150
Front seat frames	$170
Spare tire bracket	$50

Over $800 to replace these commonly missing items with ordinary reproduction pieces. Increase that amount if you want "F" marked top quality repro pieces, even more for take-off items in good condition, and even more for NOS—a LOT more! Suddenly you see why that jeep you are looking at probably was stripped in the first place; the pieces were sold off to restorers at a good profit.

Vehicle History

This is a somewhat intangible part of a restoration candidate vehicle that can affect the final value of the finished vehicle, and the selling price of the unrestored vehicle as well. The more you know about the vehicle's past, and can document it, the more valuable the vehicle is to a collector. 99.9% of the vehicles that undergo restoration simply "surfaced" on the market without any clear history. Those few WWII jeeps that have been restored that have documented history have proven to be much more interesting and desirable. We all know that the WWII jeeps that we restore began their life during the war, but where did it serve? How did it make it back to the US? Did it ever leave the US? Who bought it from the US Government? When and for how much did they buy it? What has the vehicle done in the 60 years since the war? We have all lamented at one time or another, "Oh, if the old girl could just talk." Some vehicles can "talk" via their documentation. If you find a restoration candidate vehicle with a verifiable history I would give it stronger consideration than a similar vehicle with no history.

What Will It Cost?

Prices for restored jeeps are more consistent and documented than prices for unrestored vehicles. If you are buying an unrestored WWII jeep from a collector or restorer you will most likely pay a higher price than if you buy it from the farmer down the road. If you buy the vehicle from the farmer down the road you will need to rely on your own knowledge and understanding of WWII jeeps to be sure of what you have, whereas a collector or restorer will more than likely correctly identify the vehicle and its strong points.

The cheapest WWII jeep I have ever bought was free, the most expensive one I ever considered buying sold for $5000. I have paid $250 to $400 for rusted-out parts vehicles. Most of the restoration candidate vehicles I have bought were between $1300 and $2500. This seems to be typical for a vehicle that is missing many bolt-on items and two or more combat wheels.

I currently know of a 1942 Script Ford GPW with matching numbers engine, five combat wheels, all the bolt-on stuff, nice bumper gussets and a good restorable body for sale for $3800. That is a good deal in my book. (Remember that combat wheels cost $800, bolt-ons cost $800, engine compartment stuff can cost $1200 ...suddenly the vehicle is only $1000 more than these commonly missing items!) It is disassembled in a pile and so the seller is having a hard time selling it, but for a restorer it is a good vehicle at a good price.

How do you arrive a price for an unrestored vehicle? One way is to look the vehicle over closely and list the missing items that you know you will need to buy, then go on line or look through the vendor ads in *Supply Line* magazine to add up the total cost to purchase these items. Consider this cost when you make an offer to the seller. It can give you some strong bargaining points. Consider also the Top Ten list above because the value of a vehicle goes beyond the sum of the value of its parts.

In restoring GPW 20577 I spent almost $8000 in parts and labor (machine shop, sandblaster, etc.) and GPW20577 was a very complete, solid, original vehicle to begin with. Almost everything was under the hood, it had five nice combat wheels and was missing only a couple hundred dollars worth of bolt-on items. I have detailed these costs in the appendix to give you an idea of what you are facing whether

Fig 63 – *Typical condition of an MB restoration candidate vehicle. It has the wrong windshield frame, no front bumper gussets, and no combat rims. This vehicle can be restored, but it won't be cheap.*

you restore the vehicle yourself or you have it restored for you.

Paying more for a more complete vehicle to begin with almost always ends up saving the restorer money in the long run.

Precautions, Traps, Pitfalls

Finding and restoring a WWII jeep is normally a long and expensive process. I have seen hobbyists try to cut corners and get themselves a restored jeep fast and cheap. Remember the Impossible Triangle? (Good, Cheap, Fast.) Well it holds true here, too.

Avoid the urge to purchase a post-war civilian jeep such as a cj2a or cj3a and "convert" it into a WWII jeep. What you will end up with is neither "fish nor fowl." It is not a well restored cj2a (or cj3a) nor is it a WWII jeep. You will be throwing money

away. If a WWII jeep is what you want, wait and find one to restore. If you find a nice cj2a it should be restored as a cj2a. It will be much more valuable as a cj2a than some half-baked WWII jeep "wannabe."

One way to economize on your WWII jeep restoration may be to initially "restore" the WWII jeep using less expensive 16" civilian jeep rims and without all of the bolt-on items at first. You can upgrade to combat wheels at a later time and you can add bolt-on items as finances allow. If you opt for this method DO NOT compromise on the drivetrain, frame, and body restoration. Get this done right the first time! It is easy and satisfying to upgrade your pride and joy to proper combat wheels at a later time or to add on grab handles or a canvas top, but suffering along with a poorly rebuilt engine or bad brakes for the sake of economy is not smart. Your jeep will be a disappointment to you and will be a waste of time, money, and effort. If you are hiring out the labor involved in restoring your jeep perhaps the restorer will consider restoring the frame, drive-train, and sheetmetal only. The remaining parts of the jeep, the bolt-on items, the combat wheels, the canvas, etc. constitute a large part of the cost of the jeep but can be done by the owner at a later date as finances allow.

Some restorers may be reluctant to only do a "one-half" restoration of this type because their name and reputation goes along with each vehicle they restore. This is a valid concern on the restorer's part so ask your restorer if this is an option that they may consider.

CHAPTER 3
Owning a WWII jeep

Owning a 60 year old vehicle that was built for battleground duty is, not surprisingly, quite different from owning a modern-day passenger car. Special consideration for maintenance, driving, storage, insurance, transporting, etc. needs to be considered. In this chapter I will highlight some of the peculiarities of owning one of these WWII workhorses. I will assume that the jeep you own is restored to original condition and specifications. If your jeep is modified in any way, then you may need to adjust these recommendations to fit your particular vehicle.

Maintenance

Recommended Manuals

Many WWII jeep owners enjoy collecting vintage publications that pertain to their vehicles. One popular War Department Technical Manual, TM9-803, *1/4 – Ton 4X4 Truck (Willys-Overland Model MB and Ford Model GPW)* is a "must-have" for the WWII jeep owner. It is divided into two parts. Part one is "Operating Instructions" and part two is "Vehicle Maintenance Instructions". This one manual will cover the majority of the WWII jeep owners

Fig. 64 – Two important manuals for the WWII jeep owner to have: TM 9-803 on left and SNL G-503 on right.

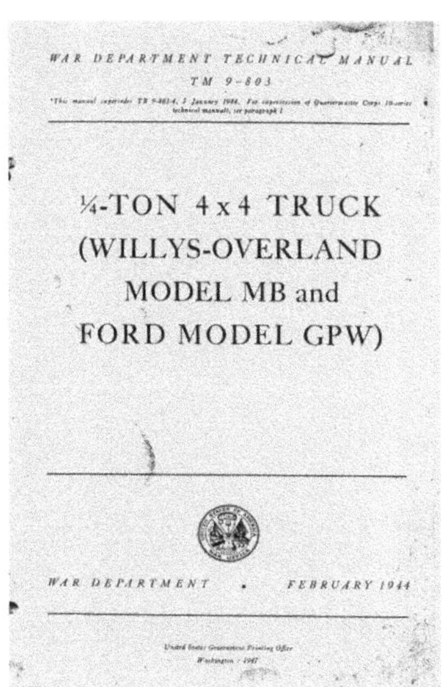

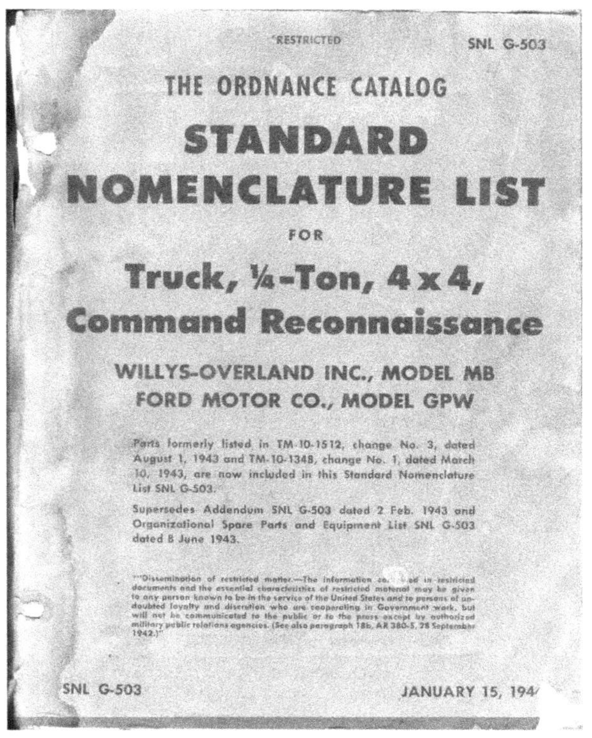

concerns. TM9-803 covers everything from adjusting the engine valve clearance to how to strap on the axe and shovel. Reprints of TM9-803 are available from suppliers such as Portrayal Press (www. portrayal.com) in a so-called three-in-one manual that is comprised of TM 9-803, TM1803A, and TM1803B. This three-in-one manual covers most every element of

WWII jeep operation and repair and sells for about $40.

Another key manual to have, especially for the jeep restorer, is SNL-G503. "G503" is the government designation for the WWII jeep, either Ford or Willys, and "SNL" stands for Standard Nomenclature List. Put these together and SNL-G503 stands for the Standard Nomenclature

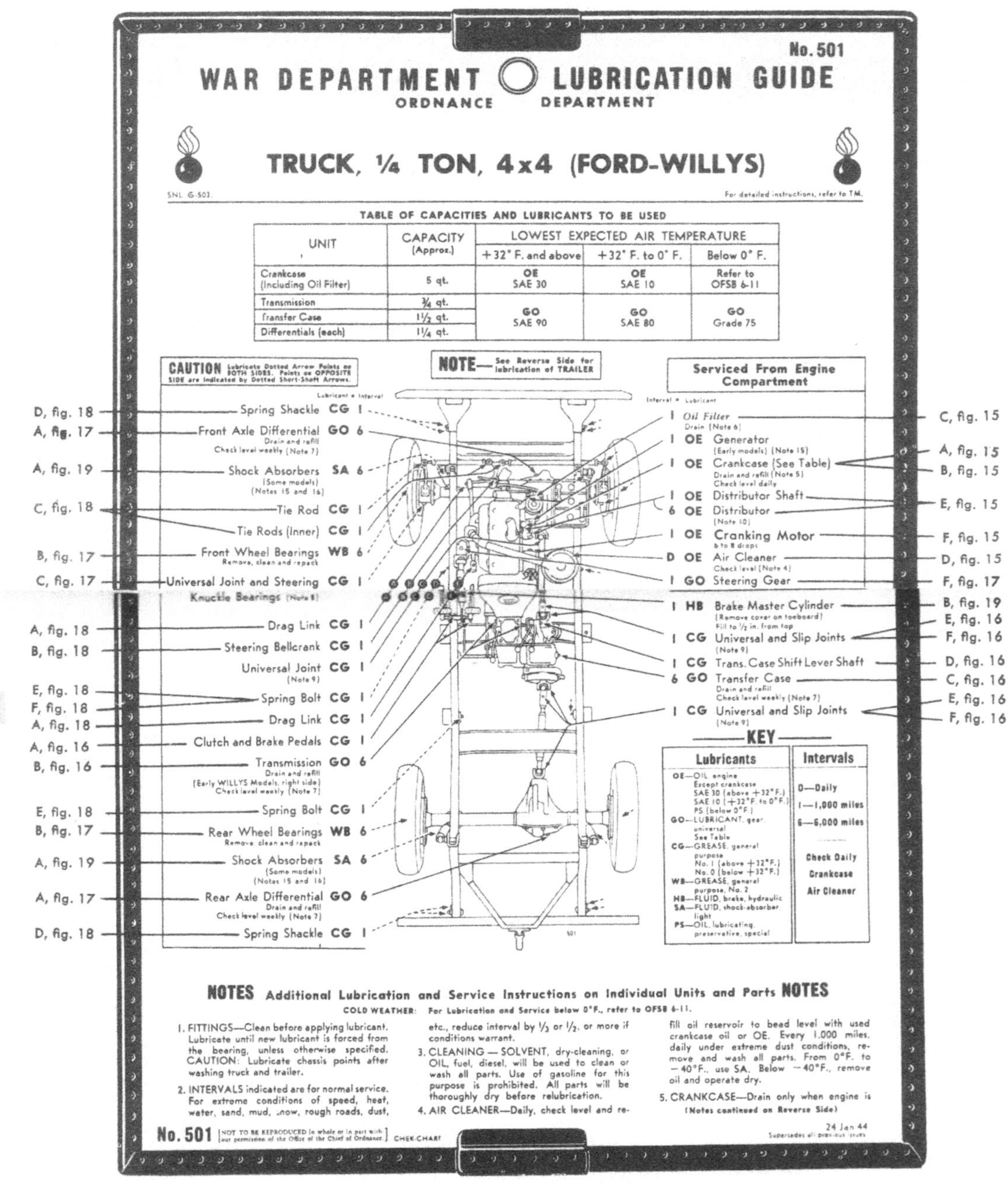

Fig. 65 – War Department Lubrication Guide No. 501

List for all WWII jeeps. It is essentially a complete list of every single part in the WWII jeep. Every nut, bolt, gasket, washer, shim, bearing, shaft, brace, bushing - you get the idea. The SNL-G503 also has many drawings, photographs and exploded diagrams of jeep components. It lists manufacturers of individual components and part numbers, both Willys and Ford numbers as well as manufacturer's numbers, too. SNL-G503 is a wonderful reference for identifying the correct part for your WWII jeep. Be aware, however, that several revisions to SNL-G503 occurred during WWII so you should get the edition that applies to your particular vehicle most closely. Portrayal Press offers SNL-G503 as a high quality reprint.

For the computer-savvy WWII jeep owners, a CD is available with TM9-803 as well as many, many more jeep related manuals in PDF format from Military Media, Inc. (www.military-media.com) for about $20. While the print version is a lot handier in the shop, the CD is certainly bargain priced considering all the manuals you get. You can print-off pages from the CD as needed and enter them into a three-ring binder "shop manual", too.

Sometimes you get lucky and can find one of these original Technical Manuals at a flea market, a used bookstore, or a military vehicle swap meet. If you do find an original manual I recommend that you carefully photocopy the original and place it in a zip lock bag for safekeeping. Put your photocopy into a three-ring binder and use the copy in your shop. The original manual is wonderful to keep as part of the jeep's original vehicular accessories (see chapter one) and you can get greasy fingerprints all over the photocopy without concern.

Bodily Fluids of the WWII jeep

It has been said that if your WWII jeep does not leak oil it can only mean one thing—you're out of oil! Well, they don't *all* leak, but a few drops here and there is neither uncommon nor cause for alarm. The trick is to follow a maintenance routine that includes checking all the fluids regularly.

Consider the following list of fluids with their capacities and you will see that opportunities for leaks abound and a routine check of all these levels does take time and effort to perform. *(unit=quarts unless otherwise noted)*

Engine crankcase oil (with filter change)	5.0
Transmission oil	.75
Transfer case oil	1.5
Front Differential	1.25
Rear Differential	1.25
Steering knuckle (each)	.25
Steering gear	.25
Air cleaner	.625
Fuel tank	15 gallon
Cooling system	11.0
Brake system	.25

In addition to the fluids listed above, the standardized WWII jeep also has 27 individual grease zerks located at various points under the chassis that require periodic greasing. Each of these grease points ooze and sling grease all over the chassis making it very hard to keep a restored WWII jeep "crispy-clean" if it is a vehicle that gets regular use.

The large number of places on a WWII jeep where grease and oil go is really only one half of the lubrication concern for these 60 year old vehicles—the other important factor is the lubrication interval for all these lubrication points. Unlike modern passenger cars, which by comparison are essentially "maintenance-free", the WWII jeep was designed to be serviced at what seems to be very frequent intervals by today's standards. Ever wonder why there are no old fashioned service stations left any more? It is because the need for

Fig. 66 *– Old-fashioned service from a WWII-era service station. Roland J. Bernier poses at his service station in 1944.*

routine vehicle service has diminished incredibly over the past 30 years. The War Department Lubrication Guide No. 501, January 1944, specifies the lubrication intervals for normal service conditions for the WWII jeep. The Lube Guide states that the 27 or so grease zerks must be re-lubed every 1000 miles, more frequently under "extreme" conditions, and after washing the vehicle. The engine crankcase and oil-bath air cleaner are to be inspected daily, and all four wheels are to be removed and the wheel bearings cleaned and repacked with wheel bearing grease every 6000 miles. This regimen is unheard of in modern automobiles and the owner of a WWII jeep needs to be aware of the fact that the technology in their WWII jeep is old and maintenance of it is labor intensive.

I was lucky enough to have in my hometown one of the few remaining old-fashioned service stations in our area. It had been a family business for a couple generations and I felt comfortable that the mechanic/owner, who also owned old jeeps, understood the special needs of my GPW. The station finally closed a couple

years ago and I resorted to doing lube maintenance on my own, but sometimes the notion of crawling on the ground under the jeep with a grease gun and rag didn't appeal to me all that much. I found myself putting off the scheduled lube jobs and "stretching" the interval. On a whim one day I drove my 1942 Ford GPW up to the nearby "Express Lube" franchise oil change place and it caused quite a stir! In fact the old jeep got first-class service from the techs at the "Express Lube" and they even allowed me to coach them into finding all of the hidden grease zerks, drain points, etc. I have since brought the GPW back and had them do complete transmission, transfer case, front axle and rear axle oil drain and replacement. I even let them change the engine oil, but I bring in my own oil filter because they do not stock the correct size on hand. The staff was surprisingly accommodating, careful and thorough. Is this true of all "Express Lube" locations? I doubt it. Are you more likely to find old-fashioned service at an old-fashioned service station? Probably, but as a WWII jeep owner you might want to stop by your "Express Lube" during a quiet time and see how they respond. If the routine maintenance is painless and quick for you it will more likely happen as scheduled.

War Department Technical Manual TM9-803 has a copy of War Department Lubrication Guide No. 501 included in it. The guide specifies the type and grade of each lubricant, the location of each lube point, and the service interval for each lube point. Lubrication Guide No. 501 is also printed on a fiberboard card that fits in a holder under the hood of late-war jeeps to serve as a reference for maintenance personnel.

Fuel and Additives

WWII jeep manuals state that the jeep was intended to operate on leaded gasoline with an octane rating of 68. Most unleaded regular fuels available in the US today have an octane rating of 87. The large difference between these two numbers is not because gasoline is much higher octane today, but due to the fact that the method used to calculate octane number has changed since WWII. There are two methods for determining the octane rating of fuels, the "Motor Method" and the "Research Method". Sixty years ago, a fuel's octane rating was determined using the Motor Method, which has more severe test conditions, and hence lower octane ratings, than the Research Method. Today a fuel's octane rating is determined by both methods and the average of the two numbers is what is shown on the pump. This average is known as the R+M/2 octane (from the calculation of the average) or as the "Road Octane Number". Either way, the net result is that the octane rating for fuel has been inflated over the years. The good news is that a WWII jeep runs beautifully on regular unleaded gas with an octane rating of 87 (R+M/2).

The absence of lead from today's fuels does not adversely affect the performance of the Go-Devil engine. Some restorers insist that in order to burn unleaded gasoline in a jeep engine, the exhaust valve seats must be replaced with hardened steel seats. Whether or not this is true is debatable, but the practice of installing hardened seats in a jeep engine during rebuild is a common one. The hardened seats supposedly can tolerate the unleaded gas better than the original valve seats. I always have hardened seats installed mostly because my engine rebuilder feels strongly about it and keeping him happy is always a good move. I am not certain that the hardened seats are necessary, but they are easy enough to install during rebuild, so why not?

Fuel additives such as lead substitute or Marvel Mystery Oil are not necessary based on my observations over many years of driving. If adding a capful of Marvel Mystery Oil to each tank of gasoline somehow makes you more comfortable by all means go ahead. These additives won't harm the Go-Devil engine in any way that I have seen—they don't seem to do much at all. One exception to the additive rule would be fuel stabilizer added to the fuel tank of a jeep being stored. It seems like a good idea. Fuel preservative may be particularly useful if the jeep is being stored in a warm location, which would promote the degradation of fuel. Here in Maine, when I put my GPW or MB up for winter storage it is in an unheated building and the cold temperatures tend to preserve the fuel so I don't use the additives myself.

Miscellaneous Maintenance Tips

The TM9-803 service manual is very comprehensive in its coverage of a WWII jeep's normal routine maintenance. There are a few maintenance issues that I would like to highlight a bit. These tips were discovered the hard way in some cases and they are listed here in no particular order.

Tire inflation is one concern. The manual says that normal tire pressure is 35 psi. I find that 30 psi gives a smoother,

Fig. 67 – An over tightened fan belt can destroy the bearings in the WWII jeep's generator. Set the belt tension as specified in TM 9-803.

more stable ride, but in either case having uniform tire pressure from tire to tire is important to insure proper handling characteristics. Remember that the WWII style NDT tires used on jeeps is a bias-ply tire, with handling characteristics that differ from the more common radial-ply tires used on modern day passenger cars. Most notably, the bias ply tires tend to "stick" to ridges in the roadway. This is particularly noticeable when exiting a highway onto an off-ramp for example. You may find that when the tires reach the edge of the main pavement they can "stick" to the low ridge and not pass off the roadway onto the exit ramp smoothly. Improper inflation can exacerbate this condition as can improper front-end alignment.

Be careful when adjusting the tension on your fan belt not to set it too tight. If in doubt set it looser than you think necessary and watch for signs of slipping. By operating the vehicle with an over-tightened fan belt you can ruin the bearings in your jeep's generator. Don't ask me how I know this.

If your WWII jeep has a tendency to overheat check the following things:

- Low coolant level
- Loose fan belt (don't over-tighten!)

- Absence of thermostat. Huh? That's right, if someone in the past has removed the jeep's thermostat its absence will cause the Go-Devil engine to run hot, especially at high speed. At first glance this seems to be backwards thinking, but apparently without the restriction of flow caused by having the thermostat in place the water pump cavitates and coolant flow is impeded. Go figure.
- Check the engine timing! An engine with a retarded spark will run hot. Oftentimes the exhaust manifold becomes excessively hot under these conditions.

If your WWII jeep is hard starting due to slow cranking check the following items:

- Is the battery fully charged?
- Are the battery cables of the proper gauge? Battery cables for modern 12-volt vehicles obtained from the auto parts store are too small in diameter for use on six-volt systems. Get proper battery cables from a WWII jeep parts or wiring supplier.
- Are the engine-to-frame ground straps of sufficient weight and are the connections "tight and bright"? Remember that the engine is mounted on rubber engine mounts, so the engine-to-frame straps are crucial. Corroded or loose ground strap or battery cable connections will cause slow cranking.

If your WWII jeep cranks normally, but is hard to start check the following items:

- Is the fuel fresh and clean? Old gasoline that has been in the fuel system of an improperly stored jeep must be drained and replaced.
- Is the fuel reaching the carburetor? Try actuating the hand-primer lever

on the fuel pump several times before starting. If this improves starting you probably have an air leak in a fuel line connection somewhere causing the system to lose its prime when sitting. These air leaks are especially common on the firewall mounted fuel filter.

- Does the jeep need a tune-up? Remember, the spark plugs on your brand-new car are meant to last 100,000 miles. The plugs on a WWII jeep often need replacing annually. Same goes for the points, cap and rotor button of the WWII jeep.

Don't forget to oil your engine's distributor shaft regularly. The TM9-803 shows you where the oiler is for this item and specifies a 1000-mile service interval. I oil mine more frequently than specified just because it is easy to do using the firewall mounted oil can and I have seen what happens when a WWII jeep owner forgets to oil this part—first the shaft seizes, then the shaft snaps, then the ride is over!

Verify the dipstick marks for your engine. Do this by changing the oil and filter and adding 5 quarts of oil. Start the engine and let it come up to normal operating temperature, then check the oil level on the dipstick. You may find that the "full" mark is nowhere near the oil level at this time. This may be due to the interchanging of parts in the past or other reasons. Nonetheless, use a file to scratch a new "full" line on your dipstick at the oil level indicated and refer to this mark in the future.

Be careful when assembling the oil filter canister after changing the filter element during an oil change. Be sure that the gasket is aligned and seated correctly and the cover bolt is tightened snugly. Failure to do this will result in a spectacular oil bath for your engine compartment —what a mess!

Check the brake fluid level in the mas-

Fig. 68 – *Two points of concern when performing routine maintenance: A) the oil filter cover, and B) the distributor shaft oiler.*

ter cylinder regularly. Get yourself a very long-stem funnel that can be used to fill the master cylinder from under the hood. The long-stem funnel works better than trying to fill the master cylinder through the access hole in the floorboard. Do not compromise on the WWII jeep's brake system in any way. If the system develops a leak—fix it now! I experienced a brake system failure in a WWII jeep once and it was a real attention-getter. When the brake system fails you don't just have bad brakes, you have NO brakes! The pedal goes right to the floor! Lucky for me the emergency brake worked.

Three Ways to Kill a WWII jeep

The WWII jeep is a robust and reliable vehicle, but, like everything mechanical, it has its limitations.

The first way to kill your jeep is rather obvious: improper routine maintenance. Neglecting to properly lubricate your vehicle, failure to use antifreeze in the cooling system, failure to service the brakes as recommended, and other routine maintenance shortfalls can ultimately destroy your investment. Luckily, most WWII jeep owners enjoy puttering around with their jeeps and keeping up on preventative maintenance is the best form of puttering a jeep owner can do. Get TM9-803 and follow the regiment outlined in the manual. If you do this routine maintenance your jeep will last and last.

The second way to kill a jeep is to drive it too fast for too long. These vehicles are low-geared and intended for slower speeds than many folks are accustomed to driving today. A WWII jeep seems happiest at 25 to 35 miles per hour. It can cruise all day at 40 to 45 MPH. But at 50+ MPH the engine RPM is excessive. Short bursts of 50 MPH speeds do the jeep no harm. Commuting to work every day at 50+ MPH mile after mile will kill the Go-Devil engine in short order. When driving your jeep you need to keep the speed down, not only to protect the engine, but also because the brakes, steering and suspension are really not suitable for 55+ MPH travel.

The third, and most often seen, way to kill a WWII jeep is sort of like the opposite of the second way. **The third way to end up with an unreliable, fickle-running jeep is to not drive it enough.** Sitting in storage week after week will slowly turn an otherwise wonderful WWII jeep sour. The more you drive your jeep, the better it will run. A WWII jeep that is driven every day ends up being incredibly reliable and smooth running. I am not talking about going out to the shed, starting the jeep and letting it idle for 10 minutes here either. That won't do. Regular drives over the road of about five miles or more are needed to thoroughly heat up the engine to drive off excess crankcase moisture. Turn your headlamps on during these drives to work your generator, too. These drives keep your battery fully charged, and they consume fuel, which

must be replenished keeping the fuel in your tank fresh. Frequent five mile drives heat up and dry out your exhaust system reducing rust formation in the exhaust pipe and muffler. These drives also keep the mice out of your upholstery, the spiders out of your engine compartment and the wasps and hornets out from under your dashboard.

The way to keep your jeep happy is with plenty of grease and oil and frequent leisurely drives.

Storage

Being a collector car the restored WWII jeep inevitably will spend more time in storage than the family mini-van or SUV. Some jeeps are used seasonally depending on their location, others, even those in places with year-round perfect weather go into storage occasionally while the owner is away on travel or for other reasons. Storage situations are a fact of life for WWII jeeps today, but jeeps were not designed to sit and wait. Short-term storage of a month or two simply requires a dry garage. Safe, damage-free long-term storage for three months or more requires some planning and preparation.

Moisture Effects

Moisture, high humidity, dampness—however you refer to it, it is unacceptable in a long-term storage area for your WWII jeep. The best storage area is a garage or shed that is appropriately ventilated to reduce humidity. High humidity leads to rusting and corrosion of the jeep's steel body and frame as well as to mildew and other damage to canvas tops, seat covers and safety straps. A dry garage should be your first choice. If a dry garage is unavailable, a temporary zippered canvas storage building (aka: zipper-garage) can be made acceptable. Be sure the zipper garage is situated in a well-drained area, on dry, raised pavement or a raised gravel bed if possible. If the zipper garage is set on open ground a waterproof ground cloth made of a heavy plastic tarp that fits tightly from wall-to-wall is required. Even if these conditions are met, a zipper garage needs proper ventilation to exhaust moisture that can accumulate inside it from normal temperature fluctuations. If well thought out, a zipper garage can be good dry storage, but be aware that many insurance companies will not provide comprehensive insurance coverage for vehicles stored in zipper garages. Aside from offering no theft protection, zipper garages are also ineffective at keeping out pests such as mice, squirrels and insects.

Unless you live in a bone-dry desert, storing your jeep outside under a tarp cannot provide adequate ventilation needed to prevent moisture build-up and the associated damage to the jeep. Don't do it, come up with a better plan.

Animal and Insect Damage

Preventing animal and insect damage to your jeep in storage is important in some storage locations. Mice can chew upholstery and canvas tops over a winter and completely ruin these canvas items. Cats can deter mice to some degree but they sometimes enjoy urinating on canvas seats. Squirrels and mice can nest in engine compartments and exhaust systems and cause serious damage in doing so. Wasps, hornets, bees and other insects can build nests and hives in all the nooks and crannies of your jeep.

A good critter-proof building is the best answer, but some other precautions can help. My storage shed is accessible to all the above critters so I need to take some precautions when storing my jeeps over the winter. I first remove the canvas top, windshield cover and other loose canvas accessories fold and pack them

Fig. 69 – Miscellaneous canvas items are stored in a plastic tub with moth balls. The front seat cushions are covered in plastic trash bags with more mothballs inside.

While I don't normally fog my jeep's engine for over-winter storage, I do insert the hand-crank and turn the engine over about once a month manually. This keeps the rings from sticking to the cylinder walls and seizing the engine.

into big Rubbermaid plastic tubs with snap-on lids. I throw in a few mothballs too, just for good measure. I cover the seat cushions with plastic trash bags, adding still more mothballs to each bag. I clean-out the glovebox and, yup, you guessed it, add some mothballs to the glovebox. I cover the exhaust pipe opening with duct tape and I fill a mesh onion bag with still more mothballs and set this bag on the radiator under the hood to protect the radiator welting. The mothball smell in my storage shed gets pretty strong and seems to work at discouraging mice and squirrels (as well as moths I suppose!) from moving in. Sticky-traps and D-Con poison on the floor around the jeep probably can't hurt. Follow label directions on these items.

Wasp, hornets and bees are dormant in winter months where I live so they don't molest my sleeping jeeps. Even so, I suspect that the mothballs might be pretty effective in turning them away if they did think about nesting in my stored jeep.

Fig. 70 – *Periodic charging of a battery in storage will prolong the life of the battery.*

Preparing Your jeep for Storage

1. Fill the gas tank and put "fuel stabilizer" into the gas as directed on the product label.

2. Be sure that your anti-freeze is rated for the lowest expected temperature in your climate.

3. Change the engine oil and filter if it has been more than 200 miles since the last oil change. Note that you will NOT have to change it again in the spring if you change it before storage! Use your firewall-mounted oilcan to oil the lube points under the hood as well as linkages, and the distributor shaft.

4. It is a good idea to thoroughly clean your jeep before storage. Dirt and crud that stays on your jeep for months seems a lot harder to remove.

5. You may want to "fog" your engine, especially if your storage area is likely to be somewhat damp or for extended storage periods. Fogging oils your cylinders and helps prevent engine seizure. It can be purchased at auto parts stores or also at snowmobile and marine stores. Note: Do not run your motor after fogging until ready to remove from storage.

   a. Start the engine and remove the carburetor air horn.
   b. Spray Fogging Oil into the carburetor of running engine.
   c. Shut off engine after 10 seconds (often engine will choke itself off). For additional protection you can also coat the cylinders directly in addition to steps a-c.
   d. Remove spark plugs.
   e. Attach extension tube and spray Fogging Oil into each cylinder for 3 seconds.
   f. Replace spark plugs.

6. Remove the battery and store it in a cool, dry place. Charge the battery

during storage with the appropriate battery charger once per month.

7. Check that your jeep's tire pressure is 30 to 35 psi. Even being fully inflated the jeep tires will develop temporary flat spots from storage. You will feel these flat spots as the jeep bumps down the road for the first mile or so after taking your jeep out of storage, but the flat spots will fade. Do not let the tires go flat in storage as the weight of the jeep on the rim can pinch and damage the inner-tube. For very long term storage (a year or more) getting the jeep off of its tires and up on blocks is safest for your tires and tubes.

8. Follow the procedure outlined above for animal and insect control as appropriate for your storage facility.

9. Set up a lawn chair next to your jeep and visit her often.

Insurance

Insuring your jeep differs from insuring a typical family car. First of all the insurance companies cannot simply look up the value of your jeep in a reference book so it is often the owners responsibility to document the value of the jeep by having an appraisal done. Having your jeep appraised costs about $100 and it provides you and your insurance company a detailed description of the vehicle and its value, which is critical to have in the event of a loss. Once the appraisal is completed you can purchase through your regular auto insurer an "agreed amount" policy where the insurer agrees to pay the appraised amount in the event of a total loss. This differs from a normal "stated amount" policy that you might have for your family car where the loss is adjusted to the current value of the vehicle because the insurer can look up the family car's current vale.

I have an agreed amount policy on my 1942 GPW with the company that insures my family's other cars. The agreed amount is $15,000 and the policy costs me about $600 per year. I have the jeep in storage for part of the year so my annual insurance costs are less than $600, usually about $350-$400, but there are NO RESTRICTIONS on how, when or why I drive my jeep at all. Period.

Being an antique vehicle you have the option of purchasing "Collector Car" insurance or "Antique / Classic Vehicle" insurance from several insurance companies that is considerably cheaper than regular car insurance.

Antique / Classic Vehicle insurance for my $15,000 GPW was quoted at about $160 per year—considerably less than the normal agreed amount policy that I have —so what is the catch? Restrictions of course!

There are restrictions on the total number of miles the jeep can be driven in a year. There are age restrictions on the driver (oftentimes a minimum age of 26 years). There are storage and use restrictions, too.

Lets see what an actual "Amendatory Endorsement" form that you must sign when you get one company's Antique / Classic Vehicle insurance form says...

The "Antique / Classic Vehicle" insurance will provide coverage for the following uses:

a. Occasional pleasure driving
b. Exhibitions
c. Club Activities
d. Parades
e. Other driving not in violation of the provisions listed below:

Coverage will not apply when the insured vehicle is used for:

a. Backup transportation
b. Errands (i.e. grocery runs, trips to large shopping centers)
c. Driving to or from work or school

d. Business or commercial purposes
e. Utility use which includes towing, hauling or off-road use
f. Participation in, practicing or testing for any racing, speed contest, time trial or track event

Coverage will also not apply unless:

a. The insured vehicle is kept in a fully enclosed, locked, permanent-structure garage facility when not in use
b. The vehicle is not driven more than the annual mileage limitation (usually about 2500 miles per year)

If you can live with these restrictions, then the Antique / Classic Vehicle insurance can save you a lot of money. The companies offering this insurance are reputable and responsive, but the limitations are real. If you drive yourself to work in your restored WWII jeep one day and someone steals it from the parking lot, don't expect a check in the mail from your Antique / Classic Vehicle insurance provider.

Another insurance option to ask your agent about is "Recreational Vehicle" insurance. Some owners in certain areas of the country qualify for this type of insurance and it seems to be a good value. There are fewer restrictions than with Antique / Classic Vehicle insurance, but it may not be available or economical to the owner of a single WWII jeep in your area.

I enjoy driving my WWII jeeps as often as possible. I drive them to work, I go off-road, I go on errands with them. Some years I might drive 4000 miles. If my family car is in the shop, I might drive the GPW instead. Clearly, Antique / Classic Vehicle insurance is not for me! I bite the bullet, pay for the normal insurance, and sleep well at night knowing my GPW is covered.

Transporting

Having the ability to transport your jeep long distances safely and quickly can make a wide variety of fun activities possible. Whether it is participating in a large parade or car show in a far-off city, getting to the trail-head of an off road adventure or attending a military vehicle rally in a neighboring state, driving your jeep these long distances is sometimes impossible. There are a few ways to transport a jeep over long distances and I have tried several of these way over the years. The first of these ways is simply flat-towing.

Flat-towing involves attaching a tow-bar to the front bumper of the jeep and hauling it with all four wheels on the ground over the road. This method

Fig. 71 – Somewhere on I-295... A GPW makes its way from Maine to Maryland for the annual MVPA East Coast Rally.

causes the most stress in the towed jeep's steering, suspension and drivetrain not to mention the front bumper and those precious bumper gussets. It adds miles to your jeep and wears your tires. The jeep also must be insured and registered to be flat towed in most states. By disconnecting the driveshafts or pulling the drive axles, you can limit the amount of wear the jeep's transmission and transfer case experience, but steering and suspension still wear. In addition to the stress and wear on the towed jeep, the towing vehicle also has to be able to safely control and stop the towed jeep all on it's own. You cannot back-up a towed jeep any distance so the driver of the towing vehicle must plan ahead when pulling into parking lots and such. Auxiliary towing lights can be purchased which attach to the towed jeep and are powered by the towing vehicle to increase safety. I do not recommend this method of towing, but in a pinch it will work and can be done. I'd give this method one star out of four. (*—)

A second method of hauling your WWII jeep is by using a tow dolly. These dollies are available quite reasonably from rental centers and towing your jeep using one is far superior to flat towing. The tow dolly carries the jeeps front wheels off of the ground minimizing stress on the steering and suspension and the dolly has its own tail lamps and turn signals for added safety. The jeep is secured to the dolly by straps that bind to the front tires so there is no unusual stress on the front bumper or gussets. The rear drive shaft can be disconnected for very long trips to limit the wear caused by the spinning rear wheels, although for trips of under 200 miles simply putting the transfer case into neutral seems adequate. Towing a relatively lightweight WWII jeep on a tow dolly results in a fairly stable and controllable towed load. Again, backing the tow vehicle with a jeep on a dolly is difficult, but easier than backing a flat-

Fig. 72 – *The electric trailer-brake controller unit installed on the instrument panel of the tow vehicle.*

towed vehicle by far. In some states the jeep must be registered and insured to be dolly-towed legally. I'd say two stars for this method (**—).

The next method is the one I use, carrying the jeep on a open transport trailer. Stability and control are excellent. Wear and stress on the jeep is zero. Backing is a snap and, because the trailer has its own brakes and lights, safety of towing is far superior. The drawback to this method is of course the need for a tow vehicle with sufficient towing capacity to pull the load safely. My GPW weighs 2280 lbs (I had it weighed) and the tandem-axle car-hauling trailer I have weighs in at about 1700 lbs for a total minimum towed load of about 4000 lbs. Suddenly the mini-van just won't do as a towing vehicle. (I'll give this method three out of four stars (***-).

So what is the four-star all-time most-deluxe way to transport your jeep? That would be a fully-enclosed car transport trailer. It has all of the benefits of the open trailer, but offers security and protection from the elements for your WWII jeep. Additional cargo can also be carried in the enclosed transport trailer safely and out of the weather. The drawbacks to this method include the cost, both for the trailer and for the large capacity tow vehicle needed to make it go. Something to consider regarding cost of the trailer though is that the trailer itself could make an excellent storage "garage" for your jeep. It is clean, dry, lockable and critter-proof. Keep this in mind if you need to rationalize the expense with your understanding, but long-suffering, spouse. Hauling this monster long distances will consume fuel like mad and a strong crosswind will keep you on the edge of your (driver) seat, but it is like having a magical moving garage for your pride and joy. I'll give this method four stars, if you can afford it (****).

Tandem Axles and Electric Brakes

Both the three-star and the four-star methods above involve trailers that have tandem axles and electric brakes. Tandem axles are much safer because in the event of a blow-out of one of the trailer tires, with tandem axles (four wheels total) the tow vehicle is likely to maintain directional control and effective braking better than a trailer that has only one axle (two wheels). Electric brakes on a tow trailer are also a huge safety improvement over those towing methods that simply rely on the towing vehicle's brakes to stop the towed load. In the event of a panic stop, a trailer with its own brakes is much less likely to induce swaying and fishtailing than one without brakes. Electric brakes are simple and easy to install in the towing vehicle and to operate. Most modern pickup trucks and SUVs with a factory "towing package" come pre-wired for electric brakes. All that the owner needs to do is purchase an electric brake controller

from an auto supply place and choose the correct "adapter cable" to install the controller in their particular vehicle. I installed mine in about 15 minutes and that included the time it took to mount the controller on the dashboard of the truck. To use the electric brakes they must be "set" for the load conditions on your trailer. This simply means that you load up your jeep and start off rolling slowly and applying the trailer brakes while turning up the intensity until you can feel the trailer brakes "grab". Try to remember to lower the power of the trailer brakes once you off-load your jeep otherwise the first time you stop with the now empty trailer the trailer wheels may lock-up and squeal. Follow the instructions that come with your brake controller.

Securing and Configuring Your jeep for Transport

Be -smart and careful when preparing to carry your WWII jeep on a trailer. Don't cut corners. I recall one time when I was loading up a slat-grill MB in a hurry once. My son guided me back to the waiting trailer and lowered the trailer on to the hitch ball. I then drove across the lot to where the MB waited, dropped the ramp and drove the MB up the ramp and onto the trailer. Well, my son thought I had latched the hitch and I thought he had done it and well, we were both wrong. The weight of the MB on the back of the trailer lifted the hitch off of the ball and the trailer rolled forward and into the back of my pickup truck. I carefully backed the MB off the trailer and the hitch scraped back down across my tailgate leaving a two small dents and a big scratch to remind me to check the hitch every time from now on—and I do.

In addition to actually latching the hitch, safety chains, and wiring plug, towing a jeep on a dolly or an open transport trailer requires that the jeep be secured properly and in an appropriate towing

Fig. 73 *– A WWII jeep in proper towing configuration on an open transport trailer.*

configuration. Instructions for securing the jeep to the dolly are normally provided on the dolly itself. On a transport trailer normally the dealer can offer accessory kits for securing the jeep to the trailer. I use a four-point tie-down system attaching the front and rear axles to the anchor rings on my trailer. An even better method might be web-strap type wheel bonnets that secure the vehicle to the trailer by anchoring the wheels. Most trailer dealers have all that you need available and are happy to help out a paying customer.

The preferred configuration for towing the jeep is with the jeep facing forward. This places the extra weight of the engine where you want it—on the front of the trailer. Adjust the location of the jeep on the trailer such that enough weight is pushing down on the trailer tongue to prevent fishtailing. Loading the trailer too far to the rear makes the tongue too light and causes the trailer to fishtail down the road. Remove and stow the canvas top and lower the jeep's windshield and **clamp it down**. I put bungee cords around the seat cushions of my jeep's front seats to keep them from flapping. Remove any loose objects from inside the jeep. Put the jeep in four-wheel drive, low-range, first gear and set the parking brake. Avoid covering your jeep with a tarp or plastic because on long rides flapping of the tarp will wear away the jeep's paint in spots. Any additional cargo going on the trailer like coolers, duffel bags, etc. must be tied down securely. Check the tire pressure on the trailer and on the spare tire for the trailer. Inspect the trailers stop, tail and turn-signal lights for proper operation before heading out. Test and set your electric brakes as you head out.

CHAPTER 4
Enjoying your WWII jeep

When you talk with friends or your spouse about wanting to get a WWII jeep the first response you usually get is, "What the heck are you going to do with one of those?" In this chapter we will explore that very topic! What *can* you do with a WWII jeep? Well, actually lots of stuff, much of which involves driving the jeep, so lets start by talking about driving a WWII jeep.

Safe Driving

The WWII jeep does not have many strong points with respect to driving on busy highways and city streets, but a quiet drive on a country road on a fine summer day is wonderful. So what exactly are the weak points of driving a WWII jeep in modern urban situations? Some obvious safety concerns come to mind immediately. The WWII jeep was not built with safety in mind. It lacks air bags, seat belts, roll bars, collapsible steering column, head restraints, padded dash board, even a right rear tail light and turn signals—all standard safety equipment found in modern automobiles. If driver and passenger safety are your primary concern in a vehicle, you might consider another WWII vehicle—the tank! Driving in a WWII jeep is a risky practice, but if you consider the apparent dangers associated with the WWII jeep's design, you might agree that the jeep is probably as unsafe as riding a motorcycle. In fact, given a choice, I'd rather take my chances in certain types of collisions in a WWII jeep as opposed to a motorcycle. While the jeep does lack most normal safety items it will offer a level of protection that is beyond that offered by a motorcycle. That's not saying much, but it's something.

Some restored WWII jeep owners retrofit their jeeps with basic safety equipment such as seat belts and roll bars. While these modifications can improve the safety of the vehicle they also can reduce the originality of the vehicle. I recommend that at a minimum you add a modern fire extinguisher to your list of safety equipment that you have in your jeep. I keep one in a WWII musette bag under the rear seat. It does not detract in any way from the appearance of my jeep, and in the event of a fire; it might save the day, or at least save the jeep. It is up to the WWII jeep owner to weigh the value of the safety equipment modifications relative to the loss of originality and then decide whether to install safety equipment or not.

Whether you drive a 100% original configuration WWII jeep or add some safety equipment to your vehicle, driving defensively is critically important when on the road in your WWII jeep. Leave extra room between your jeep and the vehicle ahead. Exaggerate your hand signals when turning because most people are not "tuned-in" to hand signals nowadays. Maintain a safe speed for your jeep. Remember it is a WWII jeep - not a sports car—pushing the jeep beyond its safe

Fig. 74 - *A group of WWII jeep enthusiasts prepare for an outing with their jeeps.*

operating speed to keep up with traffic is dangerous. Plan your route to avoid fast, busy stretches of road if possible. Slow down on curves and in wet weather. Be sensitive to the fact that the jeep is a slow vehicle and pull over to allow vehicles that accumulate behind you to pass every so often. Keeping a hot-headed driver trapped at 40 MPH behind your jeep for mile after mile invites him to pass you in less than ideal conditions. Pull over and let him pass before he gets frustrated. When you do pull over to let cars pass be sure it is at an appropriate spot on the road with no oncoming traffic and clear visibility. Wave the cars past you in an obvious and clear fashion so they know exactly what you are doing. Defensive driving means driving in such a way as to avoid dangerous situations. Watch your mirror, watch the road ahead and stay alert to the developing situations around

you. We should drive this way in every car we drive every day, but it is especially important to do in your WWII jeep.

WWII jeep brakes are adequate when in top condition and less than adequate when in less than top condition. Keep yours in top shape and drive defensively knowing that you will need a little extra room to stop. In a related vein, the WWII jeep's NDT tires have excellent traction on dry pavement and gravel roads. They have very good grip in many off-road conditions, too. Where the NDT tires fall short is on wet pavement and in packed snow or ice, YIKES! Reduce speed in hard rains and if you must drive on packed snow-covered roadways be extra careful.

Turn Signals vs Hand Signals

Some states require the owners of WWII jeeps to install turn signals in order to register the jeep. Most states only require

Fig. 75 – Proper hand signals according to the 2004 State of Maine Motorist Handbook.

antique vehicles to have the original equipment lighting on the vehicle. For WWII jeeps this means one single tail light on the left and no turn signals front or rear. If you are staying with this original lighting configuration you must use hand signals to communicate your intent to drivers around you. While *I* know what the signals are, how to use them, and what they mean, I find that more and more drivers today seem puzzled by my flapping and waving. Many times I signal a right-hand turn only to see the approaching driver wave back to me with an unsure look on their face. I suspect that he figures out that I was signaling a turn about one-half mile down the road. That is too late.

What can you do? Exaggerating your hand signals can help call attention to them as a form of communication and not a casual wave. You could install permanent signals in your jeep, or as a compromise you could install temporary auxiliary tail lights / turn signals such as the set I describe on my website. If you opt to stick

with hand signals, exaggerate them and stay alert. Remember defensive driving? Be sure that the drivers around you understand your intent before you proceed.

Night Driving

Driving in traffic at night with only the original lighting on your jeep is dangerous and requires a high level of defensive driving. The single, small taillight and complete lack of illuminated turn signals can be a real problem in busy traffic situations. Compound this with some rain or fog and your hand signals will become almost invisible, too. If you foresee substantial amounts of night driving with your jeep you might seriously consider a set of auxiliary taillights / turn signals.

A second concern with driving at night are the jeep's headlamps. Many restored jeeps utilize 30 watt motorcycle headlamps that are not excessively bright to say the least. Even the correct original "SeeLite" headlamps, which are brighter than the replacement lamps, cannot compare to a modern vehicle's halogen bulbs. Proper aiming is very important to get the most out of these headlamps. Refer to your manual and aim your headlamps. It is not difficult to do and can help improve night-time visibility considerably.

Security

WWII jeeps built after about October of 1942 came with a toggle-type ignition switch. No key is needed to start the vehicle, simply flip the toggle and step

Fig. 76 – Nighttime driving requires extra precautions for the WWII jeep driver.

on the starter and off you go. Even the earlier jeeps with a key type switch aren't much harder to steal because the WWII jeep has such a simple electrical system that "hot-wiring" the engine is terrifically easy. All that is needed is a simple jumper wire from the positive battery terminal to the "+" side of the coil, step on the starter and off you go again. So why aren't WWII jeeps always stolen? Well, first of all, the getaway would be mighty slow, second, the WWII jeep doesn't disappear into the crowd all that well, and third, a would-be thief probably isn't smart enough to know to step on the starter anyhow. If you are concerned that someone might accidentally or purposely start your vehicle you can open the distributor, remove the rotor button and pocket it. Without a rotor button the jeep cannot start - period. The rotor button can be removed and replaced without tools and it fits nicely in your pocket. This is an old WWII motorpool trick that eventually failed as GIs looking to "borrow" a jeep began carrying extra rotor buttons in their pockets. It is not likely that someone who happens upon your jeep would by chance have a spare rotor button in their pocket nowadays though. Another popular motorpool trick was to install an eyebolt in the dashboard of the jeep in such a position that when the jeep was shifted into reverse, the shift lever was close enough to the eye bolt to allow a padlock to be locked around the shift lever and through the eye bolt. The jeep was now locked into reverse thus preventing an easy getaway for a would-be thief.

Driving and Operational Tips

Starting Routine

The WWII jeep with an original six-volt starting system can start reliably time after time, but each jeep needs to be "learned". By this I mean you need to find the routine that starts your jeep reliably. I have found that with an original Carter

Fig. 77 – *Another motorpool security modification. The piece of chain welded to the steering column allowed the steering wheel to be locked in place with a padlock around a spoke of the steering wheel.*

W-O carburetor the following starting routine works well for many jeeps:

Engine Hot (temperature gauge at 100 F or more)

- Ignition switch on
- No choke
- Do NOT pump accelerator
- Step on starter switch

Engine Cold (air temp 50F or more, temperature gauge shows cold)

- Ignition switch on
- No choke
- Pump accelerator to floor two or three times
- Step on starter switch

Engine Cold (air temp 20 to 50F, temperature gauge shows cold)

- Ignition switch on
- Full choke
- Pump accelerator to floor two or three times
- Step on starter switch
- Remove choke once engine starts

Engine Very Cold (air temp less than 20, temperature gauge shows cold)

- Actuate hand primer lever on fuel pump 3 or 4 times
- Ignition switch on
- Full choke
- Throttle out 1 inch (varies from jeep to jeep)
- Pump accelerator to floor two or three times
- Step on starter switch
- Gradually decrease choke once engine starts
- Gradually lower throttle to idle

You will need to experiment with these procedures on your jeep to find the best combination of choke/accelerator/throttle.

Hand-Crank Starting

If your jeep engine is in good condition and properly tuned you will find that it starts quite easily with the hand crank. We hand-start lawn mowers and chain saws, so why not jeeps? I have hand-crank started my jeeps hundreds of times with great success and I haven't broken my arm - yet. Hand-crank starting your jeep as part of a demonstration at a car show or school visit almost always brings looks of sheer surprise and wonder from young people who have never seen such an event. If you learn how to do this you will find it to be not only fun, but very reassuring to know that even in the event of a dead battery you can start your jeep and drive home.

In order to start your jeep with a hand-crank it is very important that you **be sure that your engine's ignition timing is set properly**. If the timing is set too far advanced, the engine can "kick-back" and the hand crank can cause serious injury to your hands and arms. That said, my Go-Devil is in proper mechanical condition and I have not experienced a "kick-back". Nonetheless I hold the crank with my thumbs on the same side as my fingers and I pull the crank over the top in such a way that if a "kick-back" did occur, my hand would slip off the crank and out of harms way. Follow the choke / accelerator / throttle settings outlined above when hand-crank starting. I have even hand-crank started my GPW in the dead of winter with great luck! When you hand-crank start the jeep you should stand in front of the driver side service headlamp with your right shoulder towards the front of the jeep. Crouch down and grasp the crank handle pulling it slowly clockwise until you feel compression and the handle is in the 10 o'clock position. Grab the crank firmly with the right hand with your thumb above the handle on the same side as the fingers. Grab your right hand with your left hand in the same way. Quickly pull back toward you snapping the engine "over the top" so the crank quickly goes to the 3 o'clock position. The engine will start. If it does not, slowly turn the crank clockwise until you feel compression and the handle is in the 10 o'clock position again and try pulling it "over the top" again until it starts. Usually, pulling the engine "over the top" once or twice will do. Sometimes it helps to set the throttle up one-half inch or so before hand cranking to keep the engine running once it starts.

Fig. 78 – The WWII jeep handcrank stows behind the rear seat. It isn't there as a decoration though, it really works.

This is a crank start procedure checklist that works for me:

(DO THIS AT YOUR OWN RISK)

- Set parking brake securely
- All people clear of the vehicle
- Put transmission in neutral
- Put transfer case in neutral, too, just to be sure.
- Place crank in position through bumper and into front driveshaft pulley nut
- Set the choke / accelerator / throttle as above with throttle set one-half inch or so
- Ignition switch ON
- Come promptly to front of vehicle and set the crank to the 10 o'clock position
- Snap the engine "over the top" pulling the crank to the 3 o'clock position
- Success!

Cold-Weather Driving

Winter driving in a jeep requires warm clothes, a fast metabolism and some attention to details. The jeep lacks a heater, so it also lacks the typical windshield defroster capabilities, too. Driving in freezing rain or sleet is all but impossible as visibility goes to zero quickly when the windshield ices over. Equipping your jeep with a winter enclosure can provide some degree of comfort for the driver and passengers, but it will not deice the windshield. Electric window defrosting kits were available during WWII and after the war for use in WWII jeeps. Not your normal type window defroster, the WWII jeep window defroster is an electrically heated pane of glass that mounts onto the inside surface of your windshield and is held in place with suction cups. I have seen them available for sale on occasion at military vehicle meet flea markets and in *Supply Line* magazine. While these

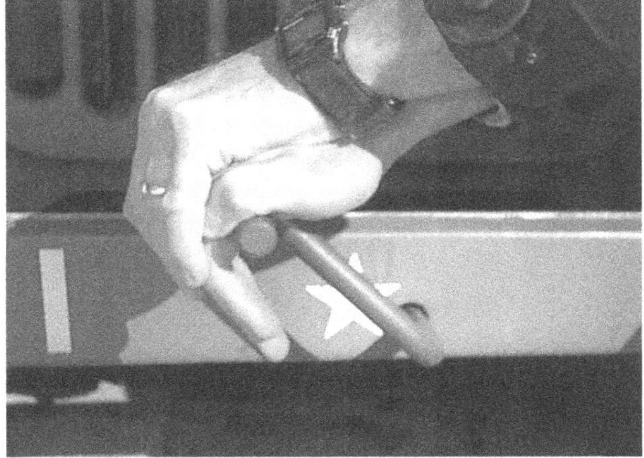

Fig. 79 – *A safer way to grip the handcrank. By keeping the thumb on the same side as the fingers and the hand cupped over the handle, the hand can slip away out of danger in the event of an engine kickback.*

Fig. 80 – *Correct stance for pulling the handcrank "over the top" from the ten o'clock position shown.*

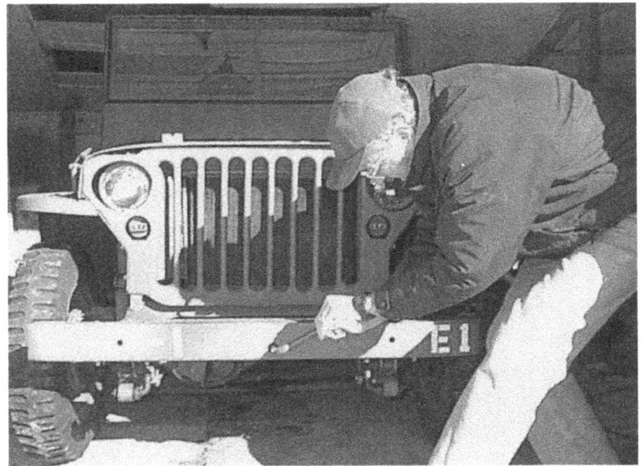

Fig. 81 – *Pulling the handcrank "over the top" towards the three o'clock position.*

defroster gizmos can be effective, in bad winter weather I just don't drive my jeep. I use the winter enclosure to extend the driving season later into the fall, but once winter sets in I put the jeep into storage. It is not only the cold weather and potential poor visibility that makes me put the jeep up for the winter, but the fact that Maine uses plenty of sand and salt on snowy winter roads. The salt used to deice roads will rust a jeep body in a hurry, so I opt to avoid these winter road conditions.

The winter enclosure restricts the driver's visibility significantly. It also makes it difficult to perform proper hand signals. Whenever I have my winter enclosure installed I also install my auxiliary taillight / turn signal set and keep my arm inside the enclosure where it is warm(er). The correct style winter enclosure that was made available late in WWII can be installed on a WWII jeep without drilling any holes in the body whatsoever. Instead of swinging doors it has door openings that zip open and flap down to allow entrance to and egress from the vehicle. The small side and rear widows are all but impossible to see traffic through and the transmission and road noise inside the enclosure gets pretty loud. On the bright side, the enclosure makes the jeep quite comfortable to ride in down to about 30F and can keep out most of the rain. The popular repro-

Fig. 82 – *Winter driving with a WWII "winter enclosure" installed.*

duction canvas suppliers all offer these winter enclosures, but brace yourself, they cost between $850 to $1200 the last time I looked.

Keeping Your jeep Active

Parades

Many WWII jeep owners participate in parades both big and small. A restored WWII jeep with its top and windshield down makes an excellent platform for carrying Veterans, Cub Scouts and other guests of honor. Being in parades is a great way to become involved with veterans in your community and it is a good excuse to give the jeep a wash job.

Becoming part of a parade usually involves a bit of pre-planning on your part. If there is a Memorial Day, 4th of July, or Veteran's Day parade in your area you should contact the local Chamber of Commerce, Town Clerk, Selectman's office or City Manager's office to see what group is responsible for overseeing the parade. Sometimes the local VFW or American Legion takes responsibility for "running" the parade. In any case the town or city officials can steer you towards the people in charge. Do this at least a month in advance and tell the parade officials that you have a restored WWII jeep and you are interested in participating in the parade. Bringing a photo of the restored jeep sometimes is helpful. If you are interested in carrying parade dignitaries such as the Grand Marshall or other honored guests let them know this too. If you contact them soon enough they will have time to plan accordingly. For most small parades this personal contact with an exchange of phone numbers is often all it takes. For larger parades there is sometimes some paperwork that needs to be filled out usually involving contact information and proof of insurance. Many parades will send you a line-up position, directions, and instruction sheets that includes pa-

Fig. 83 – *The correct WWII style winter enclosure has doors that unzip and fold down rather than doors that swing open.*

rade rules (no throwing candy from moving vehicles, etc) a week or so before the parade begins. Show up on time, dressed appropriately and ready to go. Being in the right place at the right time and ready to go will be very much appreciated by the parade volunteers who are working to get things started.

I don't like driving alone in my jeep in a parade. I feel self-conscious when I am alone in the vehicle. If I don't have a parade dignitary to carry, and it is appropriate to do so, I will ask kids to come along for a ride. Years ago I brought my own kids and their friends, more recently I will ask nephews or nieces and their friends. A jeep full of fourth graders yelling and waving surely gets the attention away from the driver and cures your self-consciousness. I limit the kid-filled jeeps to fun type parades like the local Rutabaga Festival Parade. At the more somber events such as Memorial Day or Veterans Day I prefer a quieter, more respectful cargo.

If you are carrying parade dignitaries a few items brought along can help make things go more smoothly, particularly if the dignitary is an older veteran:

Blankets: I have a couple WWII olive-drab colored wool blankets I bring along. If the weather turns cool your passenger can wrap it around his legs. If it stays warm he can fold the blanket and sit on it as the jeep seats aren't very well padded. The added height of sitting on the blanket lets the crowd see the dignitary better, too.

Water: An extra bottle of cool drinking water for your guest is smart, especially on those hot 4th of Julys. I bring water bottles in a WWII musette bag I got in a flea market. The bag looks good in the jeep and it can carry some water, snacks, tissues, etc.

A Stepstool or Box: I have some pseudo ammunition boxes in the trailer behind my jeep that I use as stepstools for the older veterans to use to get into and out of the jeep. Lend them a helping hand, too—the jeep is not easy to get into and out of. Normally the dignitary will ride in the rear seat of the jeep so you will need to help them step into the jeep and make their way into the back.

Masking tape and string: The parade committee might want you to affix some signs to your jeep identifying your passenger. String and tape end up being hard to find at the last minute before the parade starts.

Canvas top: Yup, it just might rain. Be prepared for it with the canvas top and some towels.

Driving in a parade is different from driving in rush-hour traffic even though the pace is roughly similar. Here are a few pointers that I have found helpful over the years:

Go slowly. This may seem obvious, but we tend to drive as though we have somewhere to be; however when in a parade, it is the trip that matters, so slow down. If someone steps out for a picture of the jeep or passenger-dignitary, stop and let them get a good shot. You've got no place you need to be, so why not stop?

Leave plenty of room between you and the vehicle/ band/ group in front of you. Crowding the parade entrant in front of you makes it hard for the crowd to see your jeep and passenger. Leave plenty of room in front of you so that the jeep and its passenger are identifiable as an individual entrant as opposed to the tail of the entrant ahead of you.

Pick your spot! If you can choose, avoid being placed in front of a fire truck! I was stuck there once and the fire truck

Fig. 84 - WWII jeep and trailer loaded with kids for the local 4th of July parade.

blew its horn and siren all through the parade. What a headache I had by the end of the day! Try not to follow horses; you know why. The best entrant to follow is a high school band or Shriners riding go carts or some other entrant that stops periodically and performs. It gives you a chance to stop and watch the show in front of you and talk with your passenger and people in the crowd a bit. If you are carrying the Grand Marshall or some other parade dignitary you may not have any choice of where you are placed, so be it. If you can choose your placement though, heed my warnings about fire trucks and horses. I learned the hard way on both. I also try to carry a parade dignitary whenever possible. It gives you a better position in the parade. Avoid being grouped with "Antique Cars" because these guys seem to drive along too fast and you just get lost in the crowd.

Use Low Gear, Low Range. This requires you to engage four-wheel drive due to the transfer case interlock. Some guys fear running their jeep along the dry pavement in four-wheel drive, but at the slow speeds of a parade, the torsional stresses built up in the drive train due to the lack of "slip" between front and rear axles has proven not to be a problem for me. With the jeep in "low-low" it idles along at walking pace nicely without having to slip the clutch. If after the parade you find that torsional stress has built up in the driveline and the jeep is stuck in four-wheel drive the stress can usually be relieved by backing the vehicle up about five or ten feet. The transfer case levers will un-bind and you can easily shift back into two-wheel drive high range. Some jeep owners remove the front driveshaft before a parade or they remove the transfer case interlock allowing them to select two-wheel drive low range. Still others have specially machined front axle drive flanges with the splines cut out to allow free-wheeling of the front wheels. I don't bother with any of these modifications and I have been in about three to five parades a year for many years without driveline damage.

Showing Your jeep

There are two types of official showing that I want to discuss: showing your jeep in local car shows and having your jeep judged and shown at regional military vehicle meets.

Local car shows can be a fun activity to enter your jeep in and it can prove to be a good way to find jeep parts, jeep manuals, other jeeps and jeep enthusiasts, and WWII veterans in your area. I have found all of these by being in local car shows. Many local car shows have a small entry fee for vehicles being shown. You arrive unannounced at the show site, pay your fee, set up your display vehicle and then hang out all day while the other entrants and the public (who also pay a small fee to attend) wander past your jeep and look it over. Usually the other entrants (and you) are asked to vote for their favorite vehicle in each class as they wander around and at the end of the afternoon, the winners in each class get a trophy to take home. Here are a few pointers about local car shows:

Arrive early so you can get a good spot—perhaps one with better visibility or maybe even some shade. Being the first vehicle in the row is a great spot. Take up lots of room when you park. This sometimes makes the volunteer show organizers mad because they want to pack the display vehicles in like sardines, but hold your ground and say that you need the extra space for your "display". Having room around your jeep makes it more visible and accessible to the public.

Choose your "class" carefully. You will find that there is not normally a class that your jeep fits into because it is an unusual vehicle. The show organizers tend

Fig. 85 – *On display at a local car show. The sign on the hood says that it is "OK to touch this jeep". Having a Bantam jeep trailer adds to the display and gives you a place for all that WWII gear you accumulate.*

to want to put the jeep into the "special interest" class because "special interest" really means "miscellaneous". You may find yourself in with a pretty strange bunch of vehicles in this class. It is not always a bad class to be in but you tend to be stuck out at the fringe of the show site. I prefer to be in a more mainstream class. Some shows have a class for jeeps and this is of course the best one to enter. Other good classes are antique trucks or 1940's antiques. Whichever you are assigned, try to be put in a mainstream class if possible.

Make an informative display sign. Keep it short, one side of one page maximum and have an image or two on your handout to increase interest. Have a few short, clearly identified sections (mine has a "General History", "This Vehicle's History", "Restoration", and a "Trivia" section.) At the end of your sign, point out an interesting feature of your jeep to return the reader's focus to the vehicle on display (see appendix 5). I have this sign mounted on a felt covered board that stands on an easel next to the jeep.

Let people touch your jeep. OK, you may not want to, but I encourage people to touch my GPW. I even have signs that say "It is OK to Touch this Vehicle". After walking down row after row of shiny chrome beauties that are plastered with signs warning everyone that that they are not worthy enough to—heaven forbid— *touch* the car on display, happening upon this very different looking vehicle, the WWII jeep, that is OK TO TOUCH sets your jeep apart from the crowd even further. Lets face it, what harm can likely come to your jeep if someone were to touch it anyhow? It was built to withstand the rigors of war, for Pete's sake, so let the guy touch it! The "OK to TOUCH" sign ends up being a frequent conversation starter and can make the whole interaction with the crowd more enjoyable. Remember that if you want to forbid public touching of your jeep that is certainly your right, but you may miss out on a whole bunch of fun and the risk to your jeep is minimal.

Bring food, drinks, a folding lawn chair, sunscreen and more drinks. Usually the venue you will have is shadeless and hot. There are normally drinks and refreshments for sale at the show if you would rather. Bring a pencil, note pad and maybe a clipboard for carrying your ballot around. The note pad is good for taking names and phone numbers of people you will meet who have an "old jeep behind the barn you might be interested in". I also bring masking tape for my "OK to TOUCH" sign and registration card.

Showing your jeep at regional MV meets is different from showing your jeep at the average local car show. This is particularly true if the meet is being run by a Military Vehicle Preservation Association (MVPA) affiliated club and you are intending to have your jeep of-

> *Lets face it, what harm can likely come to your jeep if someone were to touch it anyhow? It was built to withstand the rigors of war, for Pete's sake, so let the guy touch it! The "OK to TOUCH" sign ends up being a frequent conversation starter and can make the whole interaction with the crowd more enjoyable*

ficially judged. Official MVPA vehicle judging involves very close examination of your vehicle by knowledgeable and trained judges. The level of competition between vehicles present is sometimes astoundingly good (though not always) and the amount of attention to detail that is required sometimes leaves the first-time vehicle owner surprised. That said, having a vehicle officially judged can offer restored WWII jeep owners excellent feedback and advice on how to improve the quality of their restored vehicle.

Remember that no restored vehicle is perfect and that the goal of MVPA judging is to improve the quality of the vehicles the MVPA is associated with and to better preserve and symbolize a part of history.

Fig. 86 – *WWII jeep judging lineup at a regional military vehicle meet. At this meet six restored WWII jeeps were judged side-by-side.*

Vehicles are accurately and fairly judged against the official publications pertaining to that vehicle's configuration (TM9-803, SNL-G503). There are three classes of vehicle judging at MVPA meets: Restored Class, Master Class and Motorpool Ready Class. Restored class vehicles are those vehicles restored and maintained in factory fresh condition and are equipped as they would be as delivered from the Willys or Ford factory during WWII. These beautiful jeeps should not show wear, dirt or road grime and should appear to be brand new. Master Class is a competition category for those vehicles which have already attained a level of achievement in the Restored Class. The Motorpool Ready Class is for restored WWII vehicles that are accurately restored to represent a vehicle as it would appear in use during WWII. Mixing of Ford GPW and Willys MB parts on one vehicle is tolerated in this class as is a certain degree of wear, dirt and road grime. Non-factory installed WWII equipment may also be installed in the Motorpool Class Ready WWII jeep, such as radios, wire spools, anti-decapitation devices, etc. The equipment must be appropriate and accurately installed.

Unlike local car shows, where all entrants are "judged" by the attendees, you can opt to enter and show your WWII jeep at a military vehicle meet without having it officially judged. Many people bring their military vehicles to these meets to show them in the vehicle display area and do not enter them into the judging competition. These meets are excellent places to connect with other WWII jeep enthusiasts, to visit jeep parts vendors and to find that "treasure " in the flea market / swap meet area. There are often scenic rides that you can participate in with your jeep as well as trail rides and other events. Many of these MV meets last two to four days with a large variety of activities planned for each day. Attending one of these large regional meets with your restored WWII jeep is a tremendous amount of fun and a great way to learn more about your jeep and make friends in the hobby.

Trail Riding With Your WWII jeep

First and foremost let me point out that there is trail riding and there is trail riding. To some folks, trail riding means enjoying the challenge of battling your way across an impossible terrain of mud, stumps, boulders and steep embankments. Then there are guys, like me, who enjoy traveling with my WWII jeep through the woods on easy dirt or gravel access roads that offer only minor challenges of an occasional beaver-dammed culvert or minor washout. Traveling slowly along a remote woods road with the top off and the windshield down offers you incredible visibility, fresh air and the WWII jeep crawls along very, very quietly quite often allowing you to sneak up on wildlife. Whichever flavor of trail riding you choose you will find that the WWII jeep is capable and well-suited to either. Because I prefer the less challenging type of trail ride I will offer my advice regarding this. If you are interested in the more challenging type of off-road experience you will want to find a club in your area emphasing the challenge. A place to look might be through the Jeep Jamboree website (http://jeepjamboreeusa.com).

Easy trail riding is best and most safely done in groups. Taking a trail ride with another WWII jeep is fun and safer than going alone. If you experience a break-down in a remote area, having a buddy there with a second vehicle can be a life-saver. If you are traveling over access roads that experience at least some other traffic during the day, then going alone is reasonably safe, but you need to keep in mind that you might be doing some hiking or long-term waiting. Remember, too, that you may find yourself at the mercy of strangers if you experience a breakdown

Fig. 87 – *Rough terrain like this is no problem for a stock WWII jeep.*

in this type of area. The places I go on extended trail rides do not have cell-phone service and AAA is out of the question. There is, however some traffic during the day so that if I did break down, a ride out should only involve a couple hour wait for a good Samaritan to pass by. I have been lucky and have not ever had to resort to begging a ride out, because my GPW has not let me down. Is it all luck? Probably not. Some of my success is from planning. Here are some tips that you might consider whether you are heading off the beaten path with another jeep as a companion or on your own:

- Maintain your vehicle! Be sure that you have done all the routine maintenance as specified in TM9-803 before you leave on your trip. Check fan belt, tires, battery, and generally inspect your vehicle thoroughly as a precaution.

- Bring extra fuel. Your jeep has a gas can carrier on the back (unless it is an early MB or GPW) so fill the can up before you leave. Bring oil and pre-mixed coolant too (although in summer-time water will work as coolant in a pinch).

- Bring some spare parts. The original WWII list of spare parts (see chapter one) is well thought-out and I bring it along, but I also bring new ignition points, condenser, rotor button, a spare (long) oil filter line, a can of radiator stop-leak gunk, some aviator type radiator hose clamps, about 3 feet of neoprene fuel line, a few feet of electrical wire, a few nylon cable ties and some duct tape just for good measure.

- Bring the tools listed in the original vehicular accessory list (see chapter one). I also bring vice-grips, needle-nosed pliers and large pump pliers (channel-lock pliers). It is interesting to note that you can leave your Phillips-head screwdriver home because there are NO Phillips-head screws in an authentic WWII jeep. If your restored jeep has Phillips-head screws anywhere it is due to a restoration error! Bring along a saw to clear branches and small trees from the pathway and a water container of some sort. The old WWII style folding canvas bucket is just right to have along, but any similar item will do.

- Rope. During WWII, the jeep often was supplied with about 25 feet of one inch manila rope that can commonly be seen in vintage photographs wrapped around the front frame horns / bumper. This length of manila rope had eyes spliced in each end. You, too, should bring some rope along, whether it is the GI one-inch eye-spliced manila, a modern nylon towing strap or simply a coil of heavy nylon rope. It comes in handy over and over.

- Radio / cell phone for communicating between vehicles and beyond

- First Aid / survival kit / food / water / map / flashlight /extra clothes and other contingency supplies as deemed appropriate for the climate, terrain and degree of remoteness.

- File a "flight plan". Let someone know where you are going and when you can be expected to return.

Plan your ride, don't take unnecessary risks, be careful and enjoy one of the most fun activities that you can participate in with your WWII jeep.

Fig. 88 *– A "corduroy road" means slow going, but is no challenge for the WWII jeep's off-road capabilities.*

Museum and Educational Activities

Promoting the military vehicle hobby is something we all need to work at whenever possible. Public opinion can influence legislation that can affect the hobby. Furthermore, by educating the public about our vehicle's important historical contributions and development, we can help insure that our dwindling supply of restorable vehicles are valued for what they are and not scrapped or otherwise wasted.

I am fortunate to have a wonderful transportation museum in my region that offers many opportunities to get involved. The museum has several meets during the season that I bring my jeep to. In addition to summertime meets, the museum offers a winter workshop/lecture series that includes topics ranging from restoration techniques to vehicle histories. I currently have my WWII Bantam jeep trailer on loan to the museum and have had my GPW on display at the museum in the past. So what does this mean to you? Well, I strongly recommend that you visit any transportation or WWII museums in your area and consider becoming involved. If you have a restored WWII jeep you may find opportunities to use your jeep in museum related events. If you are looking for a WWII jeep, being involved in a museum can expand your contacts in the area and could lead to a connection with a vehicle for sale.

Another effective way to promote the hobby and expand your contacts in your area is to become involved in educational programs in local schools. Let local schools know that you have an important piece of WWII history available for visits. Study up on the history of your vehicle and WWII in general and learn about the production effort on the home front. Offer yourself and your jeep as a resource to American History classes and for other special class projects as needed. Be aware that public schools are very sensitive to the presence of weapons on school

Fig. 89 – *Smooth gravel access roads are a pleasure in a WWII jeep.*

grounds and let the schools know that your display may include the jeep and WWII artifacts but no guns, knives, handgrenades, ammunition, etc. If you have these weapon-type artifacts in your collection, be accommodating to the school's concerns and remove them from the collection before visiting. My experience has shown that students are fascinated with the jeep and my collection of WWII "stuff" that fills my Bantam trailer. The students I have interacted with in the past were respectful of the equipment and asked insightful and interesting questions. I have thoroughly enjoyed my visits—you might, too.

A third aspect of involvement that you might consider is becoming involved with a WWII re-enactor group or living history group. You may like to learn more about living history groups in particular as this seems like a really good way to get involved with some individuals who know about WWII and to display the GPW in an accurate way. A search of the internet yields dozens of sites with more information on WWII reenacting and living history groups.

Military Vehicle Groups and Clubs

If you did as I recommended way back in chapter two and joined the MVPA you will receive *Army Motors* and *Supply Line* magazines. In the back of each issue of *Supply Line* is a listing of MVPA affiliated groups listed by location along with addresses and phone numbers. You may look through the list and see if there is a club in your area. These clubs are like individuals in that they vary widely in "personality". Some clubs are very active and structured with large member rosters and ambitious event calendars. Some are smaller and low key. With luck, you can find a nearby club that matches your personality and meets your expectations. While membership in an MV club certainly is not necessary in any way if you own a WWII jeep, many jeep owners enjoy the camaraderie and involvement in the group. It does expand your contacts in the WWII jeep community and most groups sponsor several club activities and meetings throughout the year.

A current listing of MVPA affiliated groups can also be found on the MVPA website at www.mvpa.org.

Interacting with Veterans

Perhaps one of the most rewarding benefits to owning a restored WWII jeep is the opportunity one gets to react with WWII veterans face to face. I have met and talked with scores of WWII vets over the years and have heard amazing stories of courage, fear, danger, dumb luck and awe from these otherwise ordinary men from my community. The WWII veterans are growing old, averaging over eighty years old today. Listening to their stories first hand is a privilege that we soon will lose. Use your WWII jeep to your advantage to get out and meet these amazing men and women before it is too late. Listen to their stories. Ask them about what the war was like for them. You will find that for the most part they are happy to share their amazing tales with you. You may want to take notes or record interviews, but this is a jeep book, so I am going to explain how I am using my jeep to preserve a few of these men's memories.

Fig. 90 – *A WWII veteran gets the "ride of honor" as Grand Marshal in the local Memorial Day Parade.*

I stole my idea from a military vehicle collector I have come to know who lives in Pennsylvania. He has an incredible collection of WWII vehicles and is truly one of the "good guys" in the hobby who is always happy to share what he knows and to help out his fellow MV enthusiasts. He has a big WWII van trailer that he painted and marked up as a Red Cross van. He brought this trailer to major WWII veteran gatherings around the world and asked veterans to sign the trailer with a paint pen and to write a short message about their role in WWII on the trailer. The trailer now

Fig. 91 – *Signatures and messages left on the jeep by the past five Grand Marshals of the local Memorial Day Parade.*

is completely covered in signatures and is a marvelous tribute to the men and women who signed it. It is fascinating to wander around the trailer and read the veteran's messages.

Well, I don't have a large trailer, but I do have a WWII jeep. Furthermore it has become a bit of a tradition for me to carry the Grand Marshall of the Memorial Day Parade in my hometown. The Grand Marshall each year is a different WWII veteran from our area. I have carried six of these veterans in this parade to date. Last year I decided to begin my own tradition of having them sign my jeep. I contacted the remaining five veterans (one gentleman had passed on since his parade) and asked if they would mind signing my jeep for posterity. I was unsure how they would react to the request, but I was pleased to find that they felt "honored" to be asked to sign the jeep. I made an appointment to meet each of them at their home and I removed the windshield so they could write more easily on the inner windshield skin. I allocated each veteran about an eight inch wide piece of the windshield skin and gave

them a paint pen. My instructions were simple. I told them that some day the jeep would most likely end up in a museum and I would be honored if they would sign it and leave a message. I also prepared a scrapbook with the parade flyer about each of the men and included a picture of them riding in the jeep in the parade. The scrapbook goes with the jeep when it is on display to explain the signatures on the windshield. I chose the inner area of the windshield skin because this part of the jeep is protected from weather and is easily masked-off in the event of a re-paint of the jeep. A further benefit of this location is that it is visible to passengers and me in the jeep as I drive. I am reminded every time I ride in the jeep of the veterans and their stories told to me during the parade and after.

I was very reluctant to begin this jeep-signing project. Would it look weird on the jeep? Would the veterans think it to be a dumb idea? Would people looking over the jeep at shows feel it was corny or disrespectful? Would the jeep no longer look authentic? Well, now that a year has

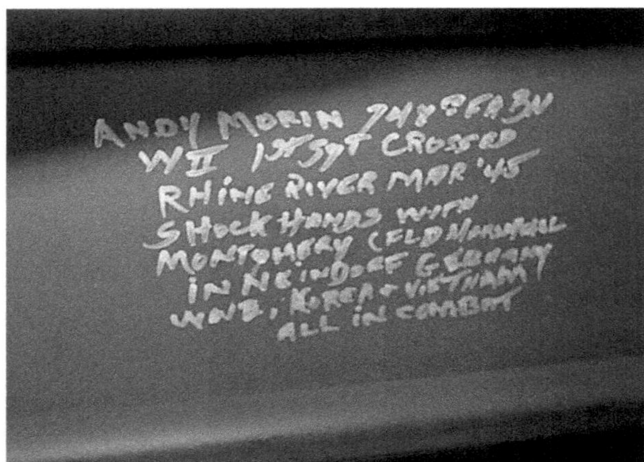

Fig. 92 – Major Andrew Morin's message (see Fig. 90).

passed since I began the project I can honestly say that I wish I had started earlier. The veterans are very enthusiastic about signing the jeep. I get only very positive feedback from people who see the signatures at shows. The signatures do not seem to detract from the authenticity of the jeep to me. In fact, the signatures seem to lend a degree of approval from a group who's perspective of WWII jeeps is one that I can only imagine: the men and women of WWII themselves.

Am I saying you should do just like me and have veterans sign your jeep? Absolutely not. What I am saying is that you should consider using your WWII jeep to interact with WWII veterans now, while you can. The day is fast approaching when no more WWII veterans will survive. It would be a shame to let them pass your jeep without telling you about "when we were driving a jeep across a wooden bridge during the Battle of the Bulge when suddenly…"

Fig. 93 – Don't pass up the chance to hear a veteran's story about what happened on this bridge…

APPENDIX

MB Serial Number by Production Year
Note: number ranges are approximate

    1941   MB100001 – MB108598
    1942   MB108599 – MB200022
    1943   MB200023 – MB293232
    1944   MB293233 – MB402334
    1945   MB402335 – MB459851

GPW Serial Number by Production Year
Note: number ranges are approximate

    1942   GPW1 – GPW90000
    1943   GPW90000 – GPW171000
    1944   GPW171000 – GPW 243000
    1945   GPW243000 – GPW277896

MB Serial Number by Style
Note: number ranges are approximate

Slat-grill MBs	MB100001 – MB120000
Early MBs	MB120000 – MB170000
Mid-production (pure Willys) MBs	MB170000 – MB280000
Late-production (composite bodied) MBs	MB280000 – MB459851

GPW Serial Number by Style
Note: number ranges are approximate

Early (Script) GPWs	GPW1 – GPW50000
Mid-production (pure Ford) GPWs	GPW50000 – GPW165000
Late-production (composite bodied) GPWs	GPW165000 – GPW277896

Appendix II

WWII jeep Tub Features

Numerous detail changes occurred over the course of MB and GPW production from late 1941 through August 1945. Darryl Deppe, of Washington, compiled many of the changes made to the MB and GPW tubs and organized the following chart which can be used to determine what features are expected to be found on any particular vintage MB or GPW.

Keep in mind that change dates are approximate. If your particular MB or GPW's date of delivery falls very close to a change date shown on the chart, then your jeep may or may not have that particular feature. The chart is an excellent reference tool for those examining a jeep to buy whether it is a restored jeep or a potential restoration candidate vehicle.

(chart on next two pages)

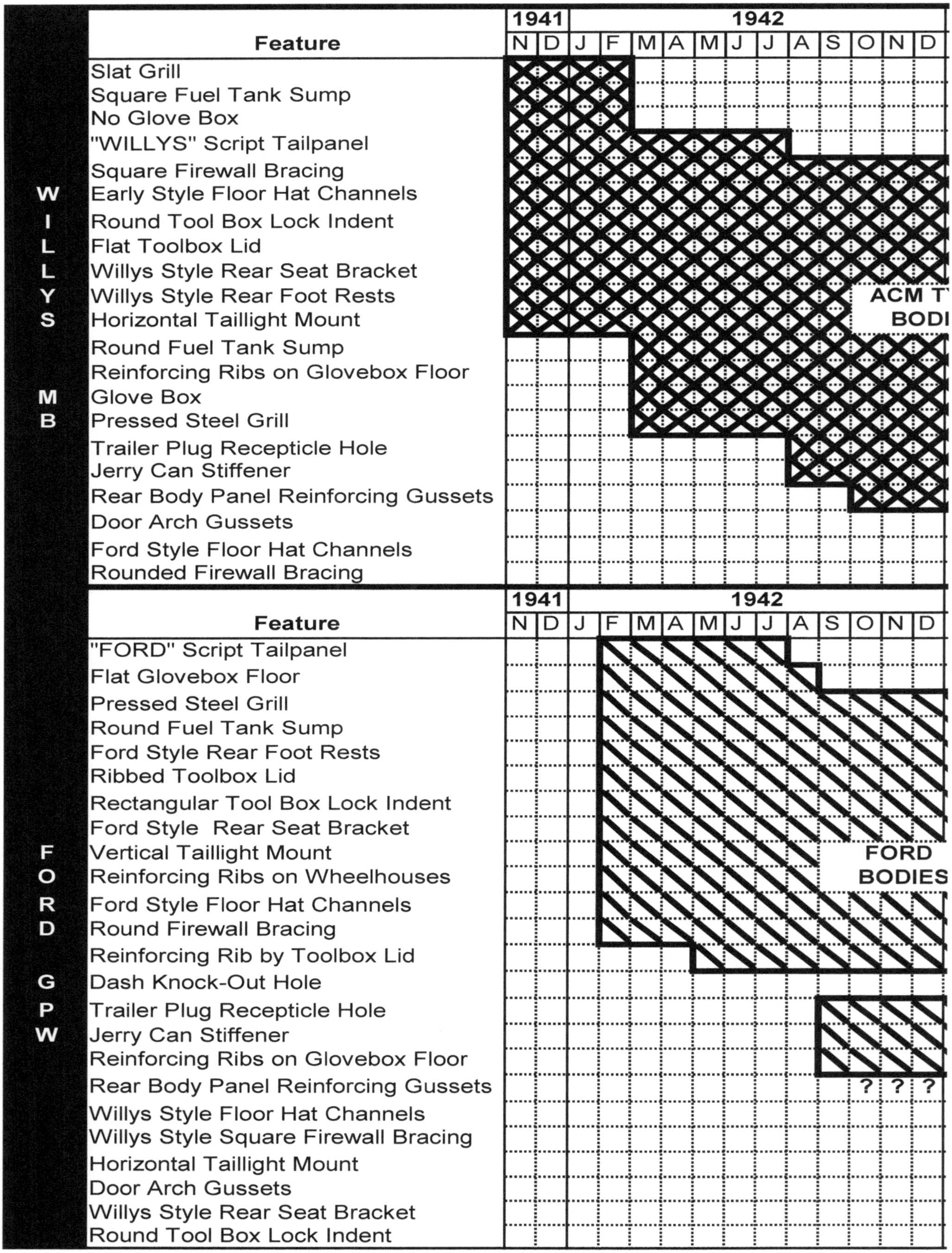
WILLYS MB
Feature
1941
1942
N D J F M A M J J A S O N D
Slat Grill
Square Fuel Tank Sump
No Glove Box
"WILLYS" Script Tailpanel
Square Firewall Bracing
Early Style Floor Hat Channels
Round Tool Box Lock Indent
Flat Toolbox Lid
Willys Style Rear Seat Bracket
Willys Style Rear Foot Rests
Horizontal Taillight Mount
Round Fuel Tank Sump
Reinforcing Ribs on Glovebox Floor
Glove Box
Pressed Steel Grill
Trailer Plug Recepticle Hole
Jerry Can Stiffener
Rear Body Panel Reinforcing Gussets
Door Arch Gussets
Ford Style Floor Hat Channels
Rounded Firewall Bracing
ACM T
BODI
FORD GPW
Feature
1941
1942
N D J F M A M J J A S O N D
"FORD" Script Tailpanel
Flat Glovebox Floor
Pressed Steel Grill
Round Fuel Tank Sump
Ford Style Rear Foot Rests
Ribbed Toolbox Lid
Rectangular Tool Box Lock Indent
Ford Style Rear Seat Bracket
Vertical Taillight Mount
Reinforcing Ribs on Wheelhouses
Ford Style Floor Hat Channels
Round Firewall Bracing
Reinforcing Rib by Toolbox Lid
Dash Knock-Out Hole
Trailer Plug Recepticle Hole
Jerry Can Stiffener
Reinforcing Ribs on Glovebox Floor
Rear Body Panel Reinforcing Gussets
Willys Style Floor Hat Channels
Willys Style Square Firewall Bracing
Horizontal Taillight Mount
Door Arch Gussets
Willys Style Rear Seat Bracket
Round Tool Box Lock Indent
FORD
BODIES
? ? ?

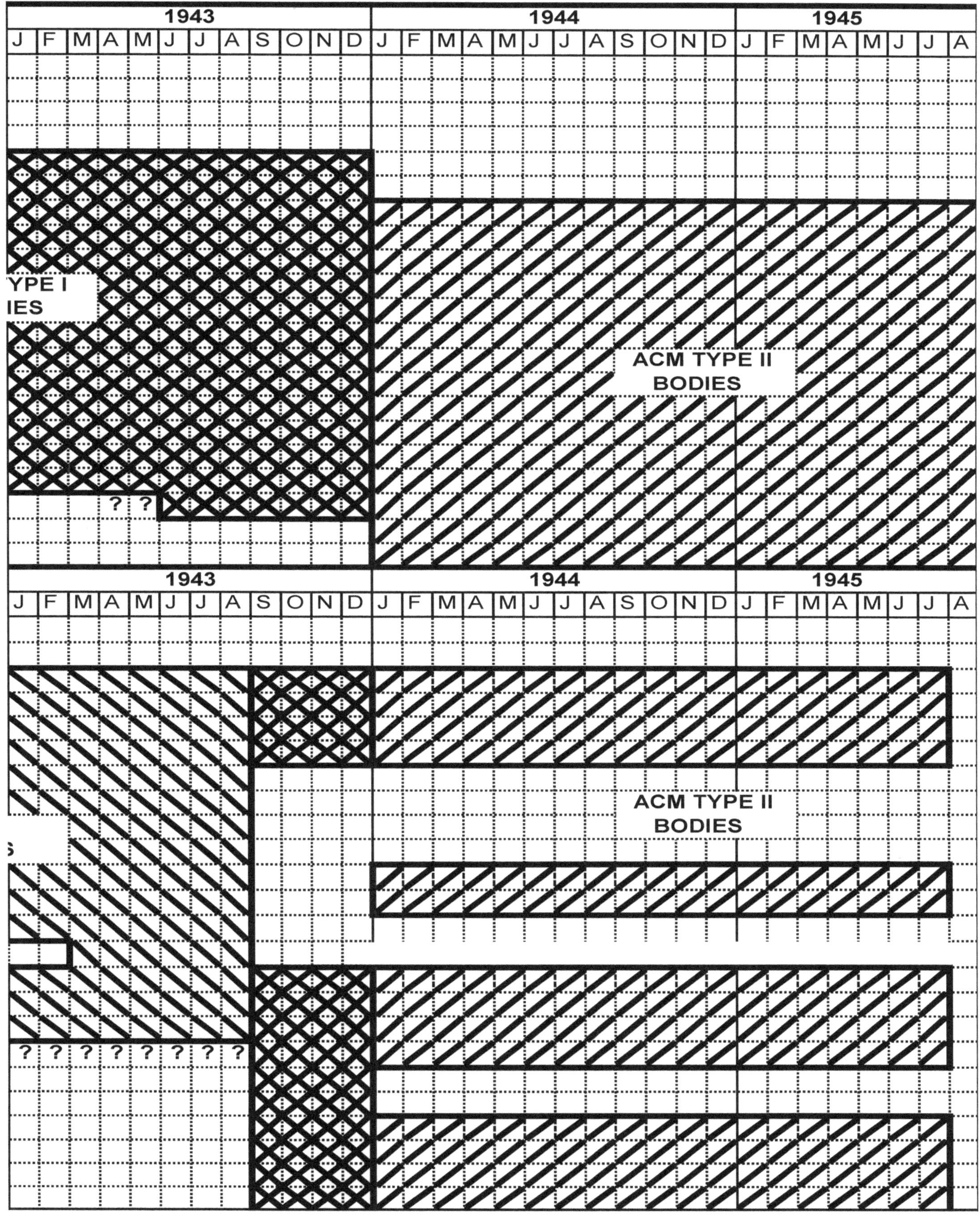
1943
J F M A M J J A S O N D J F M A M J J A S O N D J F M A M J J A
1944
1945
TYPE I
IES
? ?
ACM TYPE II
BODIES
1943
J F M A M J J A S O N D J F M A M J J A S O N D J F M A M J J A
1944
1945
ACM TYPE II
BODIES
? ? ? ? ? ? ?

There are many interesting and well-done books and websites available concerning the WWII jeep. Searching Google or Amazon.com, visiting the MVPA website and contacting military vehicle publication specialists such as Portrayal Press (973- 579-5781) or Victory Publishing (888-428-1942) will give you access many more books and websites than are listed here. I have selected just a few of the more popular books and websites that have been particularly helpful or interesting to me for this short list.

Books

All American Wonder, Vol. I & II by Ray Cowdery.

The granddaddy of them all, "All American Wonder, Vol I and Vol II" are often the first books a beginning WWII jeep enthusiast gets. The books contain a wealth of information on the WWII jeep as well as many pages of vintage photos, WWII era advertisements and random jeep-related trivia. I have used information from All American Wonder for years and I still refer back to the books regularly. The books lack organization: no chapters, no index, no table of contents. There is just a lot of good info randomly interspersed between vintage photos and old-time advertisements. I recommend the books highly; just put some post-its in the book as you go so you can find stuff later on.

The Military Jeep – Model MB-GPW by Lawrence Nabholtz

Lawrence Nabholtz's book has become a classic reference for the restorer and WWII jeep enthusiast. The book focuses on the evolution of MBs and GPWs throughout WWII by presenting high-quality period photographs of the major styles of the MB and GPW and explaining, on the facing page, the important details of each photo. The book also offers important change dates, detailed serial number lists and Registration (hood) Number information. The information is logically organized, but small details are sometimes hard to locate quickly due to a lack of index.

MVPA GPW Judging Standard and Restoration Guide by Bill Kish and Lloyd White

A no-frills little book that explains in detail what is correct and what is not correct about your restored GPW. An absolute must if you are restoring a GPW. Well organized and clearly written. (We are all hoping that the MVPA gets an MB Restoration Guide ready soon!)

Jeep Genesis, The Rifkind Report, by Herbert R. Rifkind (ISBN 0 946784 95 7)

While currently out of print, this book is actually based on a report about the development and procurement of the jeep under the Quartermaster Corps that was written in 1943. It is an interesting eye opener about the politics of the day and the struggle of Bantam Car Co. to retain hold on its "baby": the WWII jeep. Dry reading in places, but well organized and interesting for the jeep history buff.

Websites

www.g503.com
An excellent site with informative message boards, a super serial number list, technical information and up-to-date event listings.

www.g503.com/jeepdraw
The JeepDraw website. Many detailed technical drawings of the components of WWII jeeps. If you need to know where the correct hole locations are for the rear panel of your jeep for example, this is the place to go. Amazing work by Jon Rogers of Australia.

www.mvpa.org
The Military Vehicle Preservation Association official website with member information, a bookstore, MVPA judging information, and affiliated group and club listings.

www.rensjeep.com
The author's website with information on how to make an auxiliary tail light set, detailed restoration images, community involvement ideas, how to fold and store your canvas top, a virtual trail ride, etc. The website is meant to complement this book.

Appendix IV

Solid disc wheels, lug nuts and wheel studs.

All WWII standardized jeeps were equipped with two-piece bolt-together combat rims except for the first 20,700 "Slat-grill" MBs delivered. These very early "Slat-Grill" MBs were delivered with solid disc wheels. Fig. 94 shows a 4 inch wide solid disc rim (left) and a combat rim (right) side by side.

The solid disc rim got its name because its center part lacked the vent slots we typically see in other automotive rims. The heads of the eight bolts that hold the halves of the combat wheel together can be seen.

Solid disc wheels of this type are found

Fig. 94 - *Solid disc wheel, left, and combat rim, right.*

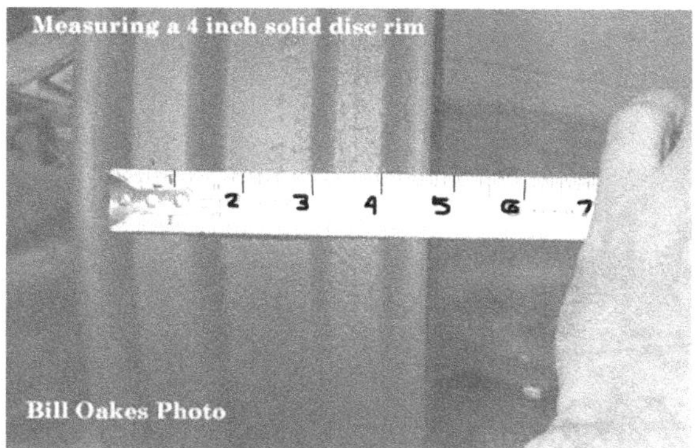

Fig. 95 – *Measuring a four-inch solid disc rim*

in two widths, 4 inch and 4.5 inch. The 4 inch wide solid disc wheels were supplied on prototype jeeps in 1941 and on the early MB's as mentioned above.

The 4.5 in wide solid disc wheels were supplied with early civilian jeeps just after WWII (cj2 and early cj2a jeeps) and also on a few "specified" MB's that were equipped with 6.50X16 tires through serial number MB120700, but there are differences.

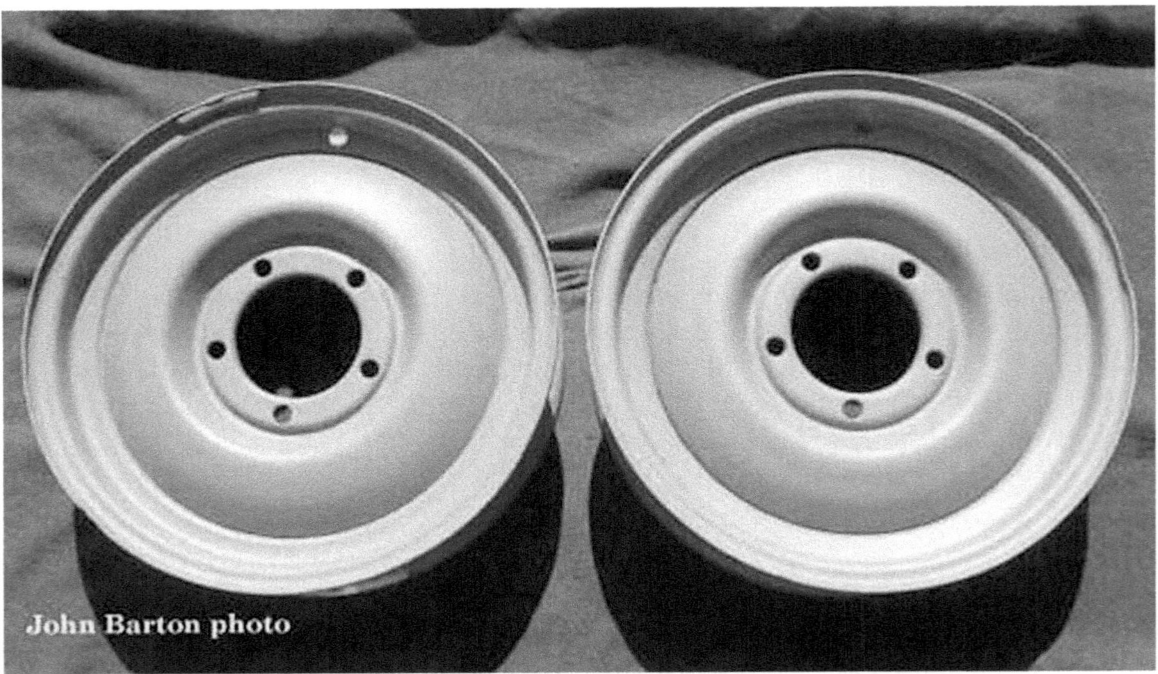

Fig. 96 – Four-inch and four-and-one-half-inch solid disc rims side-by-side.

Fig. 96 shows a 4 inch and a 4.5 inch solid disc wheel side-by-side. From this vantage point they are nearly identical, but in a side view (Fig. 97) some differences can be seen. The wheel on the left is the 4 inch; on the right is the 4.5 inch civilian wheel.

The 4.5" civilian wheel above has a "square" shoulder and a sloping shoulder just below the tire bead seat. The military version of the 4.5" rim has two square shoulders as seen in Fig. 98.

The rims are stamped. Fig. 99 shows the markings on a 4.5 inch rim dated 1946 from an early civilian jeep.

Many times the original combat rims or solid disc rims that came with a WWII jeep have been lost and later jeep wheels have been installed instead. The wheel in Fig.100 represents what is often found. This is not a "solid disc" type wheel as the vent slots are clearly visible. This wheel is from a post war cj5 jeep. These type wheels come in both 16" and 15" diameters.

The wheels are mounted to the hubs with both left-hand-thread (LH) and right-hand-thread (RH) lug nuts. The right side of the vehicle has RH threads; the left side utilized LH studs and lugnuts. The studs are normally stamped with an "R" or "L" as visible in Fig. 101.

The lugnuts themselves were normally marked in some way. Most of the right-handed ones such as those shown at the top of Fig. 102 have no markings or 3 "R"s. The left-handed ones such as those shown on the bottom of Fig. 102 have three "L"s or small notches around the edge.

Keep in mind that a previous owner may have replaced a left-side brake drum on your jeep with one from the right side of another vehicle or vice-versa. The rule of "left side of vehicle—left hand thread; right side of the vehicle—right hand thread " only applies to correctly restored or untouched original vehicles.

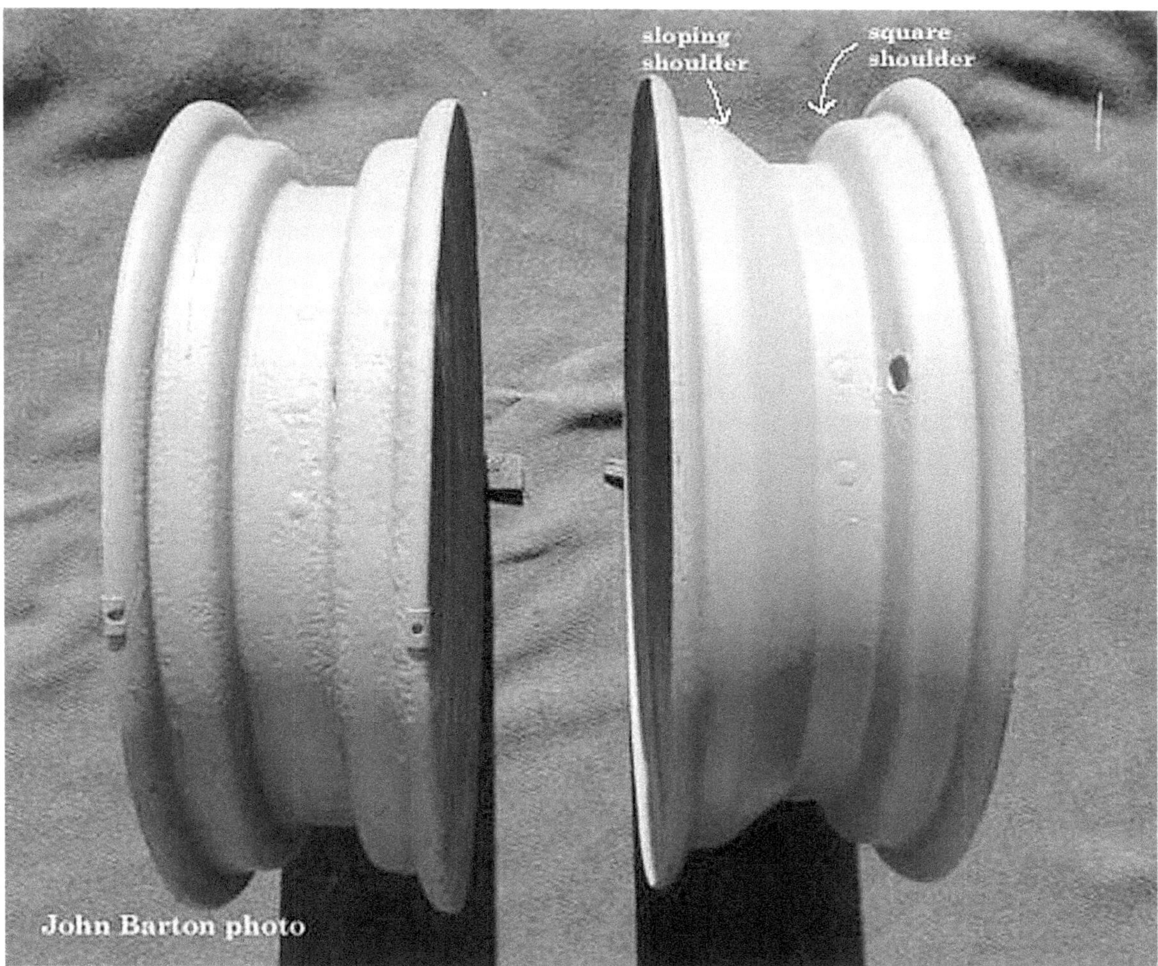

Fig. 97 – *Four-inch and four-and-one-half-inch solid disc rims side view.*

Fig. 98 – *Four-and-one-half-inch military solid disc rim.*

Fig. 99 – *Data stamping on the inside surface of rims.*

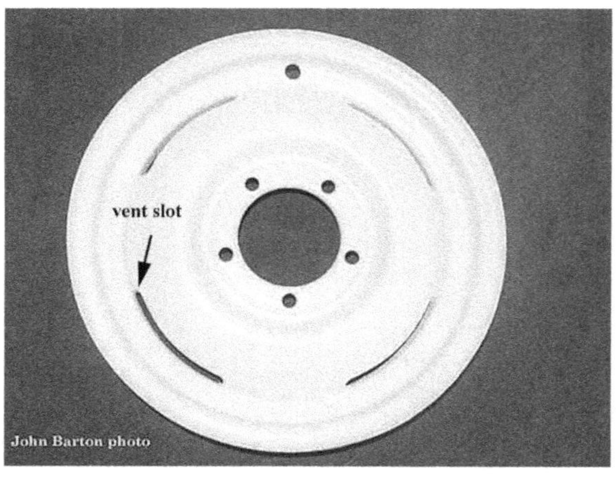

Fig. 100 *– Post-war civilian wheel.*

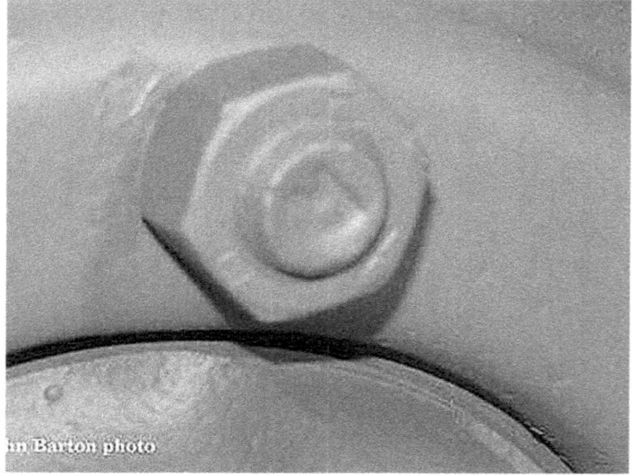

Fig. 101 *– Right-hand thread wheel stud.*

Fig. 102 *– Right-hand thread and left-hand thread lug nuts.*

Display Information Sheet

W.W.II jeep
Details
1942 Ford GPW Serial Number: 20577 Date Built: April 20, 1942

General History:

The first jeep design was a product of the Bantam Car Company in Butler, Pa. Bantam worked in cooperation with the US Army to develop the vehicle in 1940 and 1941. In the fall of 1941, just a few weeks before the attack on Pearl Harbor, the US Government awarded the first contract for standardized WWII jeep to The Willys-Overland Company of Toledo, Ohio. Shortly after Pearl Harbor, the US Government, seeing the urgent need for many jeeps, contracted with Ford Motor Company to also build standardized jeeps using the Willys designs. By the end of the war in the early summer of 1945, Ford and Willys had together produced over 500,000 jeeps.

What happened to Bantam Car Company you say? They were awarded a US Government contract to build jeep trailers...

This Vehicle:

This vehicle is a Ford-Built standardized WWII jeep. It was built on April 20, 1942, just 134 days after Pearl Harbor. It was probably delivered to Fort Oglethorpe in Georgia and used for training of soldiers there. It was sold as surplus around 1950 and was purchased by a New Jersey gentleman who drove it in Manhattan and on his property in New Jersey. The jeep's engine failed and the jeep was put in a storage shed in 1975. The owner died in 1997 and the jeep was brought to Maine by his son. This restorer purchased the jeep in 1999 and restored the jeep to its present condition. The jeep's equipment and markings portray the jeep as it would look if serving in the 47th Infantry Regiment of the 9th Infantry Division during December of 1944 (Battle of the Bulge).

Restoration of This jeep:

The restoration of this vehicle required 540 hours of restoration work . A website with over 250 picture showing the step-by-step process of restoring this jeep has been developed. Visit it at:
www.rensjeep.com

W.W.II jeep Trivia:

•You can spot a WWII jeep by the fact that it has 9 slots in its grille. Post WWII jeeps and civilian jeeps have 7 slots.

•An under-the-hood mounted oilcan is one of many design features of the WWII jeep which helped GI's service the jeep in the field.

•The word "jeep" does not appear on this GPW anywhere because the name had not yet been adopted in 1942. It was officially known as a "Truck, 1/4 ton, 4x4" at that time.

•The headlamps on a WWII jeep swing up and back to illuminate the engine to allow repairs when dark.

Appendix VI

Restoration Costs

The following list shows expenses for the restoration of GPW20577. The prices are correct for the dates listed and are no longer current. GPW20577 was an exceptionally complete restoration candidate vehicle that was missing only a very few parts and was in very sound condition. Restoration candidate vehicles that are less complete or in worse condition will require additional expenditures.

date	item	cost
7/21/99	pb blaster, tools	$15.79
7/21/99	wheel puller rental	$17.85
7/28/99	brush,degreaser	$16.24
7/29/99	sandblast	$100.00
7/31/99	paint, shackles	$95.00
7/31/99	tires	$273.40
8/5/99	envelopes, tags, markers	$10.73
8/6/99	bumper, wood filler	$71.97
8/6/99	sandblast	$25.00
8/7/99	paint	$24.15
8/10/99	hardware	$5.59
8/10/99	5/8 bit for bumper	$15.82
8/12/99	f cyl,shoes, hoses, master cyl	$214.70
8/12/99	r. brake hose	$15.00
8/12/99	clutch, disc, throwout bearing	$114.75
8/12/99	thermostat,mounts,gen bolts	$34.00
8/12/99	pinion seals,kingpin	$119.00
8/12/99	spring bolts, u-bolts, etc	$30.66
8/12/99	tie rod ends, sector repair kit	$118.15
8/12/99	mounts, snubbers synchros	$65.45
8/12/99	sm. pts. kit, gasket. & seal kit	$41.00
8/13/99	hardware	$14.74
8/14/99	nuts, armorall	$6.82
8/15/99	hardware	$1.43
8/16/99	drums turned	$12.00
8/16/99	sandblast 5 rims	$40.00
8/19/99	hardware	$3.49
8/21/99	inner tubes	$55.76
8/22/99	brake lines	$14.64
8/24/99	sandblast	$30.00
8/26/99	generator brkt spring, bushings	$13.00
8/26/99	knuckle seals, spindle washers	$29.00
8/26/99	tail light rubbers	$10.00
8/26/99	brake cylinders	$40.00

Date	Item	Cost
8/31/99	hardware	$1.49
9/3/99	paint, hardware	$13.17
9/7/99	drums turned	$12.00
9/10/99	fuel sender and gasket	$24.50
9/10/99	thermo retainer	$4.50
9/10/99	clutch rod	$8.50
9/10/99	dimmer switch	$13.50
9/10/99	starter switch	$13.50
9/10/99	fr. shocks	$35.00
9/10/99	axe sheath	$8.50
9/10/99	fender welt kit	$8.00
9/10/99	grill welt kit	$10.50
9/10/99	brake 'S'lines	$8.00
9/10/99	timing chain	$57.00
9/15/99	lower radiator hose	$13.50
9/15/99	stoplight switch	$7.00
9/15/99	driveline lock tabs	$7.20
9/20/99	driveshafts rebuilt	$63.38
9/22/99	washers and pins for shocks	$3.04
9/28/99	exhaust system	$115.00
9/28/99	sm. filler neck fuel tank	$225.00
9/28/99	sump, hat channel, riser part	$120.00
9/29/99	r. shocks NAPA# 94038	$36.38
10/1/99	harness	$250.00
10/4/99	reline brake band	$46.07
10/26/99	speedy sleeve, brake fluid	$36.24
11/8/99	welding tip	$1.04
11/8/99	acetylene/argon/o2	$44.37
11/9/99	manifold repair	$60.00
11/22/99	body supplies	$23.14
11/29/99	seat cushion set	$279.70
12/9/99	sandblast tub	$135.00
12/10/99	gen rebuild,	$81.07
12/12/99	fuel pump kit	$20.00
12/13/99	fittings, permaweld	$5.06
12/13/99	spotweld cutters, bolts	$17.25
12/14/99	bulk steel	$6.00
12/27/99	bits, blades	$14.23
1/11/00	filler, spreader	$16.51
1/12/00	sand paper	$15.87
2/2/00	grinder wheels	$19.51
2/2/00	radiator cleaning	$25.00
2/7/00	Argon/CO2 for MIG welder	$28.09
2/12/00	windshield frame	$185.00
2/12/00	t-rubber	$24.00
2/12/00	bendix drive, nos	$55.00

Date	Item	Cost
2/14/00	primer	$24.04
2/18/00	complete engine rebuild	$1,572.46
2/29/00	pad kit, junction block, pilot bush	$57.74
3/2/00	sandpaper	$26.50
3/3/00	gasket sealer, etc	$13.53
3/13/00	starter rebuild	$48.35
3/25/00	stripper, sandpaper	$21.55
3/25/00	filler,spreader	$16.51
3/30/00	spray gun rental	$8.40
4/2/00	misc hardware	$3.01
4/4/00	junction block	$15.72
4/5/00	fittings	$2.66
4/6/00	manifold planing	$28.00
4/7/00	fittings	$6.78
4/7/00	BO Drive bulbs	$24.00
4/8/00	tub attach hardware	$18.26
4/8/00	hardware, oil	$11.78
4/22/00	tune-up supplies	$34.16
4/22/00	tubing, fuel line	$24.61
4/22/00	plugs, grommet	$9.05
4/24/00	fuel line fittings	$22.17
5/1/00	washers	$1.03
5/7/00	hardware	$13.49
5/7/00	electrical	$13.39
5/15/00	steering tube, pittman arm	$130.00
5/18/00	Decal - oil filter	$6.00
5/18/00	capstan screws	$25.00
5/18/00	knobs (bo drive, panel lights)	$2.00
5/18/00	Air cleaner tube flex line	$8.00
5/18/00	air cleaner wing screw	$1.00
5/18/00	plug wire rain boot	$12.00
5/18/00	windshield to cowl rubber	$38.00
5/18/00	safety chains for thumbscrews	$20.00
5/18/00	trailer socket	$20.00
5/18/00	oil can	$5.00
5/18/00	pioneer tool - axe	$15.00
5/18/00	pioneer tool- shovel	$38.00
5/18/00	water pump	$10.00
5/18/00	clutch/brake pedal draft seal	$16.00
5/18/00	Thumbscrew - windshield	$8.00
5/18/00	Thumbscrew - top bow swivel	$8.00
5/18/00	horn contact	$10.00
5/18/00	fuel tank cap	$15.00
5/18/00	flex line -oil pressure gauge	$7.00
5/18/00	flex line - fuel line	$15.00
5/18/00	shift lever boots	$23.00

5/18/00	rubber hood blocks	$25.00
5/18/00	wipers (less handles)	$20.00
5/18/00	oil can bracket	$20.00
5/24/00	radiator hose	$19.90
5/24/00	lamps, dash	$1.97
5/25/00	paint supplies	$6.85
5/25/00	radiator cap	$6.85
5/31/00	sandblast hood, windshield, etc	$76.00
6/8/00	clamps, straps, crash pad, top	$509.36
6/11/00	oil	$15.07
6/12/00	battery bracket, horn	$107.50
6/12/00	reflectors	$28.00
6/14/00	blasting sand	$10.29
6/16/00	windshield	$38.40
6/17/00	glass bedding	$4.22
6/17/00	glass (repl broken)	$10.55
6/20/00	grille repairs	$50.00
6/21/00	primer	$6.90
6/23/00	paint supplies	$19.75
6/28/00	grease, oil	$12.61
6/29/00	front top bow brackets	$39.00

The total cost for the parts and services listed equals $7369.35. This list does not take into account approximately 500 hours of shop time I spent working on GPW20577, nor does it consider the hundreds of miles driven to get parts, the hours spent researching information and other associated activities.

Appendix VII

Restoration Journal

The following is a journal, kept in chronological order, detailing the work involved in the restoration of a WWII jeep. The jeep being restored was in exceptionally good condition when found, and was very complete.

NOTE: The journal entries below only account for actual time spent working in the shop. Be advised that hundreds of miles of driving was done to get parts and supplies. Many hours of research, and many more hours spent hunting for parts also occurred that were not included in this journal. That said, this restorer enjoys the process as much as the product. If you are involved in a restoration or considering starting one, these pages may help put things into perspective for you.

GPW 20577 dod 4-20-42
Reg# 20100234 - S
Restoration Chronology

Part One – Recovery/Documentation/ Disassembly

6/12/99 inspected jeep in Bowdoinham, Maine barn

6/15/99 jeep recovery utilizing AAA

6/16/99 initial clean-out of debris, photographing, remove front push-bar, remove incorrect top & misc. stuff. (3hrs)

6/23/99 uncover details including decal on air cleaner, F-stamps on fenders, frame #, hood number (both sides) (2 hrs)

6/26/99 remove incorrect fuel tank, remove driver seat (1 hrs)

7/7/99 move jeep into shop - all brakes frozen! engine siezed!
transmission stuck in gear! (.5hrs)

7/9/99 uncover marks on bumper, top bows, etc (.5hrs)

7/14/99 remove windshield, seats, hood, misc. bolt-ons (3.5)

7/17/99 uncover rear side star, continue disassembly (3.5 hrs)

7/19/99 remove fenders, grill, radiator, speedometer, temperature gauge, emergency brake cable, disconnect oil press line, wiring, carburetor controls, loosen steering box, remove horn contact (3 hrs)

7/20/99 remove steering wheel, remove all body bolts, remove bond straps to body (2 hrs)

7/21/99 get three helpers to remove tub and place into storage. Remove exhaust with sawzall, scrape crud and spray-down with penetrating oil (1 hrs)

7/24/99 remove engine, bell housing, skid plate, transmission transfer case, center frame cross member, front and rear axle (3 hrs)

Part Two - Repairs to Chassis

7/28/99 de-grease frame, cross-member, skid-plate in preparation for sandblasting (.5 hrs)

7/29/99 have Northeast Paint and Coatings Co. sandblast above parts

8/2/99 remove frozen left rear spring shackle from frame, repair left front bumper gusset (4.5 hrs)

8/4/99 finish left front bumper gusset (1hrs)

8/6/99 repair right front bumper gusset, bring rear axle assembly to be sandblasted, prime front bumper gussets (2hrs)

8/7/99 straighten & repair rear frame cross-member; prime and paint frame (2.5hrs)

8/9/99 remove rear axle spring u-bolts, brake backing plates, disassemble, clean and paint and reassemble right rear spring (2hrs)

8/10/99 disassemble, clean, paint and reassemble left rear spring (1hrs)

8/13/99 bring combat rims to tire shop for break-down. Clean rear differential, remove yoke, pull seal (1hrs)

8/14/99 clean and paint rear axle housing, rear brake backing plates, (needed to heat EVERY nut!) replace axle on springs and install in frame. Break-down 5th combat rim myself and save Goodyear tire. (2hrs)

8/15/99 install brake backing plate, brake shoes (rear axle) clean and Armor-All spare tire; clean rear brake drums, rear wheel bearings. Prep rims for sandblasting, prep drums for turning (4 hrs)

8/16/99 have rims blasted and have rear drums turned. Prime combat rims (1hrs)

8/17/99 paint combat rims (1 hrs)

8/18/99 clean and paint pintle hook, repair and prime bumperettes (1hrs)

8/19/99 paint and install bumperettes (1 hrs)

8/20/99 mount tires on combat rims (1.5hrs)

8/21/99 install rear differential cover, rear differential pinion seal and yoke. Clean and paint brake cylinder heat shield. Clean and paint brake and clutch pedal assembly. Weld and re-size clutch linkage hole. Install master cylinder and pedal assembly (3.5 hrs)

8/24/99 bring front axle assembly to be sandblasted. Remove springs, brake drums, brake backing plates, spindles, drive axles (2hrs)

8/28/99 disassemble, clean prime and paint front springs. Repair torque reaction spring rebound clip install springs in rear hanger bracket (3hrs)

8/29/99 remove tie rods, bell crank, steering knuckles, pinion yoke. Clean prime and paint axle housing (3hrs)

8/30/99 install axle in springs and install front spring shackles. Prime and paint all. (2hrs)

9/1/99 clean and install steering knuckles and kingpin bearings and races (2hrs)

9/3/99 clean front drive axles, spindles. (Get passenger side axle from GPW 69360) inspect and lube (4hrs)

9/6/99 clean and paint brake drums to prepare for turning. Clean and paint all brake parts (3hrs)

9/10/99 assemble left and right brakes on axle; install brake drums, inner drive axle, drive flange, etc. install steering knuckle seals (NOS. Ford) paint all (5hrs)

9/11/99 install tie rod ends, tie rods, install wheels on front axle. Do string alignment. (1hrs)

9/12/99 drain oil from transmission/transfer. Clean outside of case. Remove output flanges. Pull seals, clean and paint levers, emergency brake drum. Degrease driveshafts (3hrs)

9/15/99 bring front-end rear driveshafts to Portland Driveshaft for joints and slip inspection

9/19/99 fabricate and install front axle brake lines and hoses (2.5hrs)

9/20/99 bring emergency brake band to Gene at Morin's Auto for new lining

9/22/99 pick-up driveshafts with new joints and good slips

9/24/99 paint and install front shocks, paint driveshafts (1hrs)

10/2/99 paint and install rear shocks, exhaust pipe, driveshafts (2hrs)

10/9/99 clean, disassemble, steering gear, install new seal, gasket, and sector shaft (2hrs)

10/11/99 strip, sand, fill and paint steering column tube. Free-up manifold heat riser valve (2hrs)

10/12/99 bring manifold to Morgan's Auto Machine Shop for rebuild. Bring radiator to Topsham Radiator Shop for repair, bring engine to R&R Machine Shop for rebuild

10/19/99 clean, prime, paint drag link, pitman arm install steering box, drag link, etc. tighten tie rod ends; clean and inspect starter (3hrs)

10/25/99 fabricate rear axle and frame brake lines. Install lines; install speedy sleeve on rear transfer case output yoke (3hrs)

10/28/99 fill and bleed brake lines - one leak found and fixed (1hrs)

10/30/99 rebuild transmission and transfer case (7hrs)

10/31/99 install transmission/transfer in chassis. Attach front and rear drive shafts (use F-marked nut retainers from Ron at g503.com!) (1hrs)

11/1/99 degrease, wire-brush, and prime bell housing (1hrs)

11/5/99 pick-up radiator and manifold; paint manifold and bell housing(1hrs)

11/13/99 install transmission gasket set, install bell housing, clean, weld and resize hole in clutch tube. Clean and paint clutch linkage parts and install (2.5hrs)

11/20/99 rebuild carburetor, clean and inspect fuel pump (3hrs)

11/21/99 repair, patch, weld prime and paint and install battery tray (2.5hrs)

11/22/99 repair, weld, prime and paint oil filter bracket (4 hrs)

11/27/99 clean and paint oil filter housing (2hrs)

Part Three - Repairs to Tub

11/28/99 assemble oil filter bracket and housing. move tub into shop and begin stripping misc. items from tub (1.5hrs)

11/30/99 straighten, clean and paint axe head bracket (.5hrs)

12/3/99 clean generator case and bring to Gene for rebuild (.5hrs)

12/4/99 remove axe handle bracket, shovel bracket, harness wiring clips, air cleaner brackets, wiring terminal strips, and other firewall items. Remove oil, amp and fuel gauge, filterette (3hrs)

12/5/99 remove switches, all remaining wiring, safety strap eyebolts, windshield clamp hooks, choke and throttle controls, accelerator pedal assembly, etc. Clean switches, choke and throttle controls. Clean face of filterette. Clean accelerator pedal. (4.5hrs)

12/6/99 clean BO Drive knob, clean fill and paint F-marked taillight housing. Clean paint air cleaner bracket and circuit breaker assembly (2hrs)

12/7/99 uncover cowl "S" (.5hrs)

12/9/99 bring tub to be sandblasted. Bring blasted tub into shop and begin set-up of rotisserie (.5hrs)

12/12/99 attach tub to rotisserie (1hrs)

12/13/99 use spotweld cutter to remove rusted sump parts, driver side floor parts, inner shovel groove brace; cut floor riser rusted part. Grind off debris (3hrs)

12/14/99 cut replacement riser piece and weld in. Weld 1" piece on end of wheel house that was rusted away (2.5hrs)

12/17/99 cut away damaged floor parts, repair driver side hat channel (2.5hrs)

12/18/99 fabricate patch for floor under tank (2.5hrs)

12/19/99 weld-in floor patch. Weld-in floor strip at front of sump. Grind floor areas. Test-fit sump; test fit shovel groove brace. (3.5hrs)

12/22/99 attach groove brace, attach axe head bracket nut plate (4hrs)

12/23/99 repair filler neck hole damage, remove damaged axe sheath (4hrs)

12/27/99 fit and weld-in sump (3hrs)

12/28/99 cut tank outlet hole. Fabricate and install caged nuts for footrests (3hrs)

12/29/99 install new axe sheath, test fit tank, sump, seat. Final weld area and grind-off beads and hole fills (3hrs)

1/1/00 weld and grind drill holes on driver side (1hrs)

1/6/00 weld hole axe groove area straighten dents on left side (2hrs)

1/11/00 re-attach left rear quarter panel to wheelhouse; weld front of wheelhouse to floor riser; fabricate and install front lip of rear floor behind tank; repair left cowl tower. initial filling of front floor left side area and axe groove area (4hrs)

1/12/00 final finish and priming driver side floor area (3hrs)

1/17/00 repair, finish and prime driver side hat channel area; weld and finish holes in dashboard (3.5hrs)

1/29/00 cut away damage at right step and cowl pillar; weld patch in floor at pillar (4hrs)

1/31/00 rebuild right cowl pillar (3hrs)

2/5/00 weld patch on right step area outside; finish weld holes on right side (3hrs)

2/7/00 repair passenger floor area; weld patch in floor (4.5hrs)

2/8/00 rebuild right side floor riser, heat and remove exhaust hanger bolts. Repair right side floor beneath toeboard (4hrs)

2/12/00 weld 1" strip at front of right wheelhouse; repair rear floor riser lip. grind, finish prime area (3hrs)

2/14/00 remove damage at toeboard on right side and weld in patch. repair right step underside area (3hrs)

2/19/00 straighten dents in rear floor area. Heat and remove screws holding tool box lids. sand and finish rear floor underside; finish and prime inside front of wheelhouse (3hrs)

2/20/00 drill-out and re-tap threaded holes for glovebox door hinge. prime under dash and inside of tub. weld patch in right step (2.5hrs)

2/26/00 sandblast seat frames, jack, waterpump and fan (1.5hrs)

3/4/00 repair cowl damage. finish and prime cowl and right step; spray sandable primer in right wheelhouse interior (4.5hrs)

3/11/00 finish and prime right front quarter panel and right rear quarter panel (4.5hrs)

3/13/00 finish and prime left front quarter panel and left step (3hrs)

3/17/00 finish and prime left side (4 hrs)

3/18/00 finish and prime inside left side. Revolve rotisserie in shop to gain access to rear panel. re-sand and prime inside both wheelhouses. weld patch at passenger side of rear panel. straighten bottom edge of rear panel; grind and level patch (5hrs)

3/19/00 straighten top edge of rear panel. grind off old weld damage at spare tire bracket mount area. weld-in small patch on upper lip of hat hannel on rear panel (3hrs)

3/21/00 weld patch at driver side rear panel. weld patch in drill hole at driver side rear panel. re-align rear panel mounting brackets. weld-shut extra drill holes at left side of rear panel (2hrs)

3/24/00 weld shut all remaining drill holes in rear panel lower half; grind off all beads (2.5hrs)

3/25/00 finish and prime lower half rear panel (4.5 hrs)

3/26/00 rotate tub, remove rotisserie cross-brace and set back of tub on stands (1hrs)

3/27/00 weld-shut holes in upper half of rear panel. Weld-in reinforcing washer in rear panel hat channel at inboard lower tire mount hole. finish upper half rear panel (3hrs)

3/28/00 final sand rear panel and prime. straighten seat frames. Remove footman loops from passenger seat and prime all seat frames. Install new firewall pad (3hrs)

Part Four - Re-assembly of Vehicle

3/30/00 paint tub, fuel tank, seat frames. move chassis into shop area. clean and install valve cover on engine (engine bored 40 crank turned 20, new pistons, valve seats. bearings, valves, oil pump, etc. at machine shop) cut off long cylinder head studs. clean and install accelerator pedal linkage, oil filler tube, road vent. (7hrs)

3/31/00 install new manifold studs. install manifold. install cushions on seat frames (1.5hrs)

4/1/00 paint engine, install flywheel (turned at shop) new clutch, pilot bushing engine rear cover. install engine in chassis, attach exhaust, oil filter and bracket, oil fill tube (5hrs)

4/2/00 install water pump, clean paint and install gooseneck. strip, clean and straighten air breather crossover tube (1.5hrs)

4/3/00 weld, paint and install crossover tube. rebuild fuel pump. clean and paint rebuilt starter, generator mounts, coil mount. apply sandable primer to carburetor air horn cap. install engine retainer cable (2hrs)

4/4/00 install front generator bracket, starter, accelerator linkage. discover that incorrect (small bore) intake manifold was erroneously installed. disassemble parts manifold (MUCH HEAT needed!) (1.5hrs)

4/5/00 remove manifold, install correct intake. repaint and bring to machine shop to be planed (1hrs)

4/6/00 install manifold, carburetor (1hrs)

4/7/00 install generator, clean and paint NOS. taillight housings. clean and paint rear panel wire clips, inventory hardware needed to install tub (3hrs)

4/8/00 assemble and install taillights in tub; install accelerator pedal hinge, starter switch, dimmer switch, terminal strips in tub. (2.5hrs)

4/9/00 lube and install speedometer cable in chassis. fill transmission, transfer case, and rear differential with lube. remove shift levers. prep steering column with padding. install main wiring harness in tub. install trailer socket wiring harness in tub. install rear panel harness clip in tub. Three helpers and I lift tub from rotisserie and set on chassis. re-install shift levers while tub is loose. fabricate tub-chassis antisqueak pads (3hrs)

4/9/00 install all body mounting bolts, pads, washers, nuts and pal nuts (1.5hrs)

4/10/00 repair damaged steering tube escutcheon, clean and paint dashboard steering tube clamp. clean anti-squeak rubber and attaching hardware. make new steering tube draft seal and install steering tube (2hrs)

4/11/00 repair spare tire carrier (3hrs)

4/13/00 clean, paint and install rear panel braces, footman loops, axe and shovel brackets (2hrs)

4/16/00 install rear seat, crank clip, crank, right front seat (1hrs)

4/17/00 clean and install foot rests. install fuel tank clean, paint and install tank straps. Install driver seat (1.5hrs)

4/18/00 clean, paint and install master cylinder access hole cover, transmission floor cover. install accelerator pedal (2.5)

4/20/00 clean paint and install fuel filter. clean and paint air cleaner bracket (3hrs)

4/21/00 clean paint and install tool box lids and locks, front universal joint splash shield. install air cleaner brackets. fabricate paint and install starter anti-vibration bracket (3.5hrs(

4/22/00 fabricate, paint and install fuel line from tank to filter. Install line clips (F-marked!) and bond strap on fuel line. install plugs points, condenser, cap rotorbutton. static-time the distributor. install coil and plug wires. install battery to starter cables, clean, paint and install filterette. install oil filter oil lines (4.5hrs)

4/23/00 fabricate and install remaining 3 fuel lines (2hrs)

4/2?/00 disassemble, clean, paint and reassemble ammeter, fuel gauge, speedometer (5hrs)

4/27/00 clean, repair and paint air cleaner (2hrs)

4/30/00 paint knobs for light switches install choke and throttle controls in dash (1.5 hrs)

5/1/00 begin cleaning safety strap eye bolts (.5 hrs)

5/2/00 paint and install safety strap eye bolts. clean glove box door and data plates (1.5hrs)

5/3/00 clean, test and paint oil pressure gauge (1hrs)

5/4/00 disassemble, clean and paint temperature gauge. install oil pressure gauge and line. throttle/choke cable/ pressure line bond strap. begin installation of emergency brake handle and cable (3hrs)

5/7/00 use paint stripper to clean radiator. paint radiator (2hrs)

5/7/00 (in blast cabinet) sandblast grab handles, windshield brackets, top-bow swivel brackets, voltage regulator cover and inside of glovebox door (2hrs)

5/9/00 install radiator, finish sand and paint grab handles, top bow swivel brackets, windshield brackets. remove damaged hinge from glovebox door. remove parts hinge. dismantle 2 original reflectors. (2.5hrs)

5/11/00 clean, prime and paint reflectors. use brass cleaner to clean lenses. install grab handles and top-bow swivel brackets on tub. paint wrinkle-paint on regulator (1.5hrs)

5/13/00 spot-weld hinge to glovebox door. prime, paint and install door. install dashboard clamp hooks. install horn bracket and windshield brackets. repair, clean and paint crash pad backing plates (3.5 hrs)

5/15/00 drill-out and re-tap top bow swivel. clean, paint and install both swivels (1.5hrs)

5/22/00 install correct water pump and other misc. items that I found at Aberdeen East Coast Rally (3hrs)

5/24/00 install under-dash wiring (4hrs)

5/27/00 remove steering gear and disassemble (got new steering tube and worm) (2hrs)

5/30/00 reassemble steering gear with new tube and worm (2hrs)

5/31/00 install bond straps at firewall. install speedometer, ammeter (2hrs)

6/1/00 bring hood, fenders, windshield frame, top bows to sandblaster

6/4/00 remove rear transfer case output flange and apply RTV sealer to splines, reinstall flange, driveshaft, etc. (3hrs)

6/5/00 complete installation of emergency brake assembly (2hrs)

6/6/00 clean, paint and install dimmer switch escutcheon and draft shield. clean and install shift lever boot rings, clutch and brake pedals (2.5hrs)

6/7/00 repair hood, weld crack in hinge and brace, finish-sand and prime hood (4hrs)

6/9/00 repair right fender. straighten, weld cracks, finish and prime (3.5hrs)

6/10/00 cut damaged areas out of left fender, pound-out dents, straighten and prime top-bows (3hrs)

6/11/00 weld patches in left fender. weld holes shut; grind finish and prime left fender (5hrs)

6/12/00 remove items from windshield frame, cut-off and grind old weld damage from windshield frame, straighten top tube. (3hrs)

6/13/00 align and test fit outer windshield frame at J. Hall's. (In blast cabinet) sandblast headlamp buckets and arms, BO marker lights, BO drive light and guard, extinguisher bracket and trailer socket guard (3hrs)

6/14/00 weld-shut drill holes in windshield (20 of them) weld crack on windshield frame spread channel to allow repro inner frame to close, test-fit inner frame. (1hrs)

6/15/00 grind, finish and prime windshield frame. re-cover crash pad backing plates with new canvas and pads (3hrs)

6/17/00 prime and paint headlamp, BO drive and marker lights, repro inner windshield frame (1hrs)

6/18/00 install new wiring in BO marker lights, install new cats eyes and re-assemble (2hrs)

6/22/00 install wiring in BO Drive light and install NOS. lamp and re-assemble (.5hrs)

6/24/00 straighten, finish and prime grille, install glass in inner windshield (4hrs)

6/25/00 paint grill, fenders, hood, windshield frame; install cowl rubber on frame and install frame on cowl, install BO Marker lights in grille, install grill on frame, install crash pads, horn and inner windshield frame (8.5hrs)

6/26/00 install fenders, hood, headlamp swing-arms, hood blocks, voltage regulator, windshield frame capstan screws; clean and paint windshield holder clamps and attaching hardware (6hrs)

6/27/00 install inner windshield adjusting arms and hardware, windshield to cowl buckles, headlamps, headlamp wiring clips, left fender wiring, regulator to generator wiring, grille welting (4.5hrs)

6/28/00 install muffler, fill front differential with lube, fill crankcase, install grill welt bond straps. Install wipers (2hrs)

Start jeep at 6:01 PM on June 28, 2000 Temperature: 180 degrees Oil Pressure: 50psi @ idle Ammeter indicates charge. Let engine idle for 10 minutes and then drained crankcase and oil filter housing. Refilled crankcase and test drove for 0.5 mile.

Appendix VIII

Ten ways to identify a WWII jeep

1. **Grill** – The WWII jeep grill has nine slots as opposed to the post-war civilian CJ2A and CJ3A grills which only have seven slots. The only exception to this rule is the very early Willys "Slat-Grill" MBs which have a grill made of welded up flat bar stock.

2. **Tailgate** – There is none on a WWII MB or GPW jeep. Period. Jeeps did not come from the factory with opening tailgates until after WWII. There is no exception to this rule.

3. **Glovebox** – WWII jeeps have a glovebox on the dashboard. Post-war civilian CJ2A and CJ3A jeeps do not have a glovebox. The only exception to this rule during WWII are the very early slat grill MBs which did not have a glovebox. Also note that the 1950's M38 military jeeps have a small version of the glovebox not to be confused with the larger glovebox found on MBs and GPWs from WWII.

4. **Machine-gun "hump"** – The floor of all standardized WWII jeeps has a rounded "hump" near the center of the floor riser between the two front seats to accommodate the machine-gun mount on the frame below. No other jeeps have this machine-gun "hump".

5. **Toolboxes** – All standardized WWII jeeps have two toolboxes built into the rear wheelwells. Only standardized WWII jeeps have these two toolboxes, post-war jeeps have a single toolbox under the front passenger seat only.

6. **Fuel-tank sump** – The fuel tank on WWII jeeps sets into a sump under the driver's seat. Post-war CJ2A and CJ3A jeeps have no sump, only a flat floor under the fuel tank.

7. **Fuel filler & Pioneer tools** – The fuel tank filler on all standardized WWII jeeps can be accessed only by lifting the driver's seat cushion. After WWII, the fuel tank filler access was moved to the outside of the jeep next to the driver. This change cause the pioneer tool mounts (axe and shovel) to be deleted from the civilian jeep versions and to be moved to the passenger side of the 1950's M38 military jeeps.

8. **Full-floating rear axle** – The rear axle on all WWII jeeps is of the "full-floating" type easily recognizable by the large "hub" visible at the center of the rear wheel. Post-war civilian jeeps do not use full-floating type rear axles and have a much smaller "hub" visible.

9. **Windshield** – WWII jeeps have a split-pane type windshield that tips out at the bottom. The sheet metal "skin" below the windshield panes on a WWII jeep is plain. The post-war CJ2A has a similar tip-out split-pane windshield with a more complex tip-out mechanism and the word "Willys" embossed on the lower windshield skin. Post-war CJ3A jeeps use a completely different single-pane windshield that does not tip out.

10. **Steering bell-crank pivot pin** – The pivot pin on the steering bell crank is mounted on the front axle on all WWII jeeps only. After WWII the pivot was relocated to the front frame crossmember.

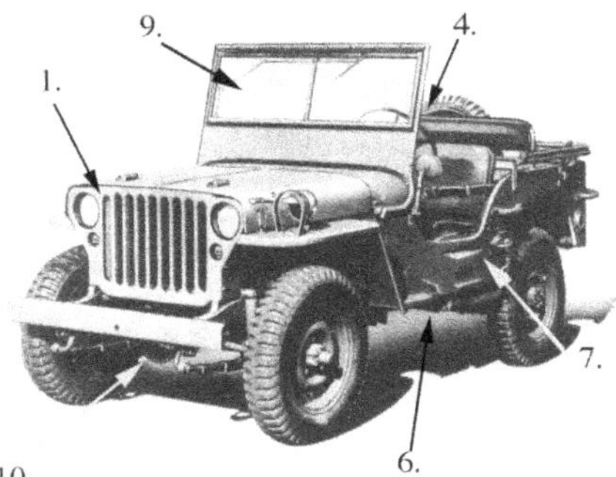

Fig. 103a & 103b – *Distinguishing features of the WWII jeep.*

INDEX